SO, YOU'RE

UK EDITION

MOVING TO

AUSTRALIA?

THE 6 ESSENTIAL STEPS
TO MOVING DOWN UNDER

SHARON SWIFT

So, you're moving to Australia?
First published in Australia in 2014 by
The Expat Concierge, a division of Tempus Lifestyle Pty Ltd
PO Box 253
Stanmore
NSW 2048

www.soyouremovingto.com

ISBN: 978-0-9924644-4-8

Cover design by Boxer & Co Pty Ltd
Page design by Ana Cosma
Illustrations by Korinna Veropoulou

Disclaimer

Whilst every effort has been made to ensure the information contained in this book is accurate and up to date, please note that the information contained here is intended only as general guidance. Laws, rules, policies and other information are subject to change and variation. Therefore, it is crucial that you carry out your own checks and due diligence in line with your specific circumstances at the time you take action. No liability or responsibility will be taken for any errors or loss, financial or otherwise, as a result of actions you have taken as a result of reading this book.

CONTENTS

So, you're a POM? Expat life in Australia   29

Step 1 : Size up   39

Step 2 : Embark   65

Step 3 : Take up residence   93

Step 4 : Tackle the necessities 125

SO, YOU'RE MOVING TO AUSTRALIA?

Congratulations! You're moving to one of the world's most desirable destinations. Like myself and millions of Britons, you've dreamt of an escape Down Under. Sundrenched dreams of white sandy beaches and breathtaking scenery. You'll be thinking of adventure, barbecues, and swapping your stressed-out lifestyle for the laid-back expat life. Your move across the world will be life-changing and unforgettable.

But there's a lot to do — so much to get organised, so much information available... Who needs another night glued to Google, trying to pull together the beginnings of a new life in a foreign country?

The truth is that any move abroad can be time-consuming and stressful, leaving you questioning the wisdom of uprooting yourself and your family, perhaps even before you've booked the plane tickets. At times like this, the Australian dream appears so much farther away than a 24-hour flight and the logistics of the move.

Having helped many professionals and their families make a successful transition to life in Australia in my role as the founder of The Expat Concierge, I have brought all of my experience into this book (a book I wish I had when planning my own move to Sydney nine years ago).

This book is the only complete reference that you will need to minimise both the thinking time and emotional stress of the seismic task of moving to Australia. Whether you are seeking to move independently, or relocating with an employer, expats-to-be need look no further than *So, you're moving to Australia?*

A little about me

Born in Singapore to a British father and Singaporean mother, some would say that, from birth, my destiny was to be a global nomad. Indeed, I spent the first 12 years of my life on the move across five continents. I was a Third Culture Kid (TCK) – defined as a child who spends a significant part of their childhood outside their parents' culture. Truth is, I didn't know any different. I was surrounded by other TCKs wherever we lived and didn't realise I was the exception rather than the norm. My relatives lived across Europe and Singapore, and our family friends were scattered around the globe due to everyone's propensity to move. At 13, we moved back to the UK so that my brother and I could spend our formative years without constantly moving. After a year off, unable to settle in the UK, my father relocated to Oman, where he worked until retirement. My mother stayed with my brother and I in the UK. We spent eight weeks each year as a family when my father returned home during our school holidays.

Once I completed my schooling, I went on to achieve an honours degree in business. As part of my studies, a third year in industry was required, and it was second nature to me to consider something away from the UK. I ended up in a beautiful part of Germany. That I had chosen to study French and Spanish and was unable to utter a word of German didn't faze me. My final year at university flew past. After achieving my degree, I set off for a job on the East Coast of the USA, just outside of New York. I just couldn't imagine settling down and living in the UK.

After 18 months, unable to secure a visa to stay in the US, I returned to London. I knew in my heart that this would be a stopgap. Knowing that there was so much of the world to be seen, I just couldn't visualise being happy in the UK and wouldn't settle until I could work out what my destiny would be. I had never set foot on Australian soil, and yet the promise of year-round sunshine, white beaches, and a laid-back lifestyle appealed. Friends and family visited and told the tales of how beautiful it was. Soon, curiosity got the better of me, and I started dreaming of an escape Down Under. The iconic images of the Opera House, the harbour, and the Harbour Bridge gave Sydney great appeal. My boyfriend, Ian, was on board with the idea, and we firmly believed we had nothing to lose by selling our house, cars, everything – to move to Sydney. That was in 2005. We are now married, both Australian citizens, and have never looked back.

My move to Australia has been the most awesome and challenging transition of my life. I love my life here so much and couldn't fathom living anywhere else. But I struggled for more than five years with the culture change before Sydney truly felt like home.

I bought all the books, researched on the internet, spoke to as many people as possible, and enlisted the help of a migration agent to help achieve our permanent residency. Ian and I decided to take a sabbatical before the permanent move and so embarked on a round-the-world trip once the visa was stamped in our passport, during which we spent a few weeks familiarising ourselves with Sydney before relocating permanently later that same year. None of this preparation, and even my experience as a seasoned expat, could have prepared me for the move. Dare I say it, I wore a comfortable pair of rose-tinted glasses and didn't truly believe that life here would be that different or require much adapting. I thought I knew what to expect and couldn't imagine how settling in could be that difficult.

I made so many mistakes when I moved here, thinking that my experience and adaptability would carry me through any of the challenges I faced. Finding a job was challenging, I couldn't stand the heat, part of our shipment was damaged, it took more than two weeks to get internet access, we had so many bad restaurant experiences, and we experienced terrible customer service over and over. When I finally found a good job, I ended up working 60 hours a week, and I wondered what on earth we had done. It couldn't have been a worse start. On the other hand, Ian took everything in his stride and wondered why we hadn't done it sooner.

Without the sense of purpose the home set-up and compliance matters gave me, I was lost. I felt guilty about having fun when I was looking for work and then felt cheated when I couldn't enjoy my free time as I was working such long hours. This was not what 'living the dream' meant to me!

My methodology and this book

This book contains all the information I wish I'd had at my fingertips when we were planning our move. I found that much of the help and advice available referred solely to the arrival and set-up in Australia. This book will take you through what to assess before you decide to leave and the pre-departure stage through to your first few months in Australia, with a focus on the five main cities of Adelaide, Brisbane, Melbourne, Perth, and Sydney. I also provide an insight into the emotions you might feel at each stage.

After giving you a flavour of today's Australia and what expat life can be like here, I will guide you through the six steps of any expat journey to Australia. From guiding you through the considerations to help you decide whether the move is right for you, I will take you through all of the steps involved in the transition, ultimately helping make Australia feel like your Adopted Home.

In my experience, any relocation involves six phases or steps that an expat will go through before they are adjusted, feel assimilated, and are less conscious of the fact they are in a new country. I refer to it as the 'S. E. T. T. L. E' process towards feeling you're settled in your Adopted Home.

There is an element of chronology in this process, but you will find that you shift between certain steps, or run through some of them concurrently. You will recognise the steps based on actions, tasks, and feelings, so don't worry so much about how long each step takes. Where sections contain many key topics or tasks, these are laid out alphabetically for ease of reference, with the exception of the key planning stage 'Embark', where I go through the stages prior to departure in chronological order.

The 6 steps to SETTLE into your Adopted Home

SIZE UP: Firstly, and crucially, I outline what you should assess and consider in determining whether a move to Australia really is right for you. Once you decide that you will be making the leap, there are your wants, needs, and criteria to assess in relation to what you want your new life to be like.

EMBARK: You're taking the plunge and there's so much to do. This section covers all of the administration and tasks you need to complete in order that your move and departure from the UK is as stress-free as possible.

TAKE UP RESIDENCE: Once you arrive in Australia, you will need to set up your home, establish a routine, and, as much as possible, replicate the essential elements of your life so that you can function and live here.

TACKLE THE NECESSITIES: It is important that you know which registrations and other essential set-up tasks you need to consider in order to be compliant.

LEARN THE ROPES: You now have a home. The next natural step is to assimilate to life here in Australia. There are a lot of subtle nuances to learn, and all of these differences will add up to a multitude of things to get used to.

EXPLORE AND DISCOVER: The next step of settling involves making new friends, feeling at ease with the Australian way of life, and becoming familiar with everything that adds up to the lifestyle you desire.

Feeling adjusted and settled means that you will relate to Australia as your Adopted Home. This end goal can take weeks, months, or even years. You will finally feel comfortable in your surroundings. The novelty of being somewhere new will have worn off and you may even start to experience the niggles and frustrations of life here. At the same time, this is when you will begin to feel a true affection for Australia and the people you have met. The journey to my Adopted Home took much longer than I expected – several years, in fact. The turning point to feeling like Australia was truly home took considerably longer – at least five years. For Ian, my husband, this all happened almost instantly. It really is a personal journey and one that I hope you achieve quickly and smoothly with the guidance I provide in this book.

THE LAND DOWN UNDER

Australia in days gone by

Before the relatively recent European settlements of the eighteenth century, Australia was settled by the indigenous Aboriginal people. Thought to have arrived here more than 50,000 years ago, they were spread all over this vast country and have a deep spiritual connection to the land.

Captain James Cook arrived in 1770 and claimed Australia for Britain. January 1788 saw the first fleet of ships bringing the famous convicts. These criminals provided labour to build public facilities and infrastructure, such as roads and hospitals, and were the bulk of the population in the first decades after settlement.

The discovery of gold in the mid-nineteenth century attracted many newcomers and settlers, and it provided the investment that built much of Sydney and Melbourne. In 1901, the states and territories formed a single constitution, one federation, and Australia as we know it today was born.

Following World War II, in an attempt to quickly build the Australian population or risk falling apart, the so called 'Ten Pound Poms' arrived. 'POMs' stands for 'Prisoners of her Majesty' and is a nickname still very much in use today for those of British descent. This was a government initiative that attracted migrants not only from Britain but from British colonies and other countries such as the Netherlands, Italy, and Greece – all part of the controversial 'white Australia policy'. These immigrants were obliged to stay and work for a two-year minimum or had to pay a large sum to return. Those that did so were known as 'Boomerang Poms'.

Australia today

Fast forward to today, and Australia is a very culturally diverse nation, with well over 200 nationalities represented amongst the migrant community, and a population of over 23 million spread over 7.6 million square kilometres.

Australia is a proud member of the Commonwealth states; its formal name is the 'Commonwealth of Australia', and it is a constitutional monarchy. The head of state is Queen Elizabeth II. The government of the six states together is a federal system, and each state has their own government. There are also three territories, which have a limited right to self-government.

Map of Australia

Lay of the land – a little snapshot

Australia is comprised of six states and three territories. The states are all on, or close to, the mainland: New South Wales (NSW), Queensland (QLD), South Australia (SA), Tasmania (TAS), Victoria (VIC), and Western Australia (WA). The main two territories are on the mainland – Australian Capital Territory (ACT) and the Northern Territory (NT), with the offshore Norfolk Island. The capital of Australia is Canberra, located in ACT.

Each state and territory has its own personality, distinctiveness, and charm. Climatic conditions, vast distances, and geography help to shape the makeup and character of each corner of the country.

Each state or territory has a capital city:

- ► ACT – Canberra
- ► NSW – Sydney
- ► NT – Darwin
- ► QLD – Brisbane
- ► SA – Adelaide
- ► TAS – Hobart
- ► VIC – Melbourne
- ► WA – Perth
- ► Norfolk Island - Kingston

AUSTRALIAN CAPITAL TERRITORY (ACT) – CANBERRA

As its name suggests, ACT is home to the nation's capital, Canberra. After federation in 1901, it was decided that a new site would be selected as the nation's capital, and Canberra was chosen. It has been said that a new site had to be chosen due to the rivalry between Sydney and Melbourne. 10 years later, ACT was declared. ACT is an area carved out in the southern part of NSW, near the Snowy Mountains. With a population of just under 400,000, most of whom live in the city itself, Canberra is the seat of the Australian Government, so it is not surprising that the Federal Government is the city's largest employer. Many national attractions are based here, such as the National Gallery and National Museum, along with government buildings and many embassies and memorials. The climate in the ACT has four distinct seasons – as it is far inland, its climate is not moderated by the ocean. Summers are hot and dry, winters can be very cold and often freezing.

NEW SOUTH WALES (NSW) - SYDNEY

Positioned in the southern half of the east coast and bordered by QLD, SA, and VIC, NSW is the most populous state in Australia, with more than 7 million people. This accounts for roughly 30% of the current population of Australia. Of this, 4.5 million reside in the greater metropolitan area of Sydney, the most densely populated city in the country. With Wollongong and Newcastle lining the coastline, NSW is the most urbanised state in the country.

NSW's capital, Sydney, is of course famous for the imagery of a city located on the water – Sydney Harbour and the ocean to the east. The mention of Sydney conjures up visions of Sydney Opera House, the Harbour Bridge, Bondi Beach, and a multitude of other beautiful beaches. There are, in fact, over 100 beaches within 90 minutes of the city. From harbour beaches to ocean and surf beaches, they are all stunning and wonderfully accessible to all. Even in the height of summer, it is possible to find beaches that are serene and unfrequented. Such is one of the beauties of living in this isolated country. Of course, it is possible to be in the hustle and bustle of popular beaches like Bondi and Manly, but venture a little off the beaten track and you may well find one all to yourself.

The main commercial centre, also called the central business district (CBD), is surrounded by a number of popular and famous sights. We have the Blue Mountains to the west, the Hunter Valley wine country to the north, and Kangaroo Valley and Jervis Bay to the south. Not to mention a number of beautiful national parks with stunning vantage points of the water and breathtaking landscapes.

With many migrants choosing to settle here, Sydney has a great cosmopolitan vibe and a diverse culture. There is a vibrant community from most corners of the world, bringing a wealth of fabulous cuisine, festivals, and communities, providing wonderful authenticity and insight. Whether it be Asian, Greek, Italian, Pacific Island, Polish, South African – find yourself in some local communities, close your eyes and you will wonder where you are. Indeed, close your eyes in some of Sydney's Eastern or Northern suburbs and you can imagine you are back in the UK!

FLIGHT TIMES TO MAJOR CITIES FROM SYDNEY KINGSFORD SMITH AIRPORT

Adelaide: 2 hours
Brisbane: 1.5 hours
Melbourne: 1 hour
Perth: 5 hours

CLIMATE AND GEOGRAPHY

The eastern part of NSW is considered relatively mild. Temperatures in summer can regularly reach 30–35°C, with the odd extremely hot day. 45°C is not usual. Summer is characterised by warm and humid days and cooler, balmy evenings. Winter can be cold, with the occasional dip below 10°C. Autumn, when the humidity decreases, is almost everyone's favourite season, and we normally enjoy mid-20°C. Spring is much the same, although with more rain.

Elevated areas, such as the Blue Mountains and the Snowy Mountains, south of Sydney, are slightly cooler and do experience snow over winter.

The southern central part of NSW, bordering with VIC is home to the Riverina region, one of the largest agricultural areas in Australia.

Within it are areas of relatively high population, with towns such as Wagga Wagga and Albury.

NORFOLK ISLAND - KINGSTON

Norfolk Island is a small island of 35km^2 located in the Pacific Ocean, in between Australia, New Zealand, and New Caledonia. The island has a population of just over 2,000 people, most of European descent or Tahitian ancestry. Its capital is Kingston, although the largest population lies in a town called Burnt Pine. There isn't a significant economy to speak of, with the main income generated from tourism. The climate can best be described as mild marine subtropical.

NORTHERN TERRITORY (NT) - DARWIN

The Northern Territory is located in the central north area of the country, the northern tip being closer to parts of Asia than much of Australia. The entire population is less than 250,000, a small number considering it is larger than NSW, with nearly one third accounted for by the indigenous peoples, the Aborigines. It is also unusual in that a large proportion of the population is located along the Stuart Highway, a major, inland road stretching from the capital, Darwin, in the far north, through Alice Springs, ending up in South Australia. In terms of climate, the state is split into tropical and humid, in the north, and desert and dry, in the central zone. Famous landmarks and tourist sites Uluru (previously known as Ayer's Rock) and Alice Springs are based in NT.

QUEENSLAND (QLD) - BRISBANE

Queensland is Australia's second largest state, occupying the north eastern corner of the country. Queensland has a buoyant economy thanks to tourism and mining and is famous for The Great Barrier Reef, which lines the east coast of the state in the Pacific Ocean. The World Heritage Site is one of the Seven Wonders of the World, visible from space, and is home to many islands, a stunning array of marine life, and wonderfully white beaches. It's truly magnificent and must be seen to be believed.

The state has the country's third largest population with just over 4.5 million, 2 million of whom reside in Brisbane – the third most populous state in Australia. Brisbane is the main commercial centre, with the Brisbane River flowing through the city, and the only Australian state capital city that is not located on a beach. Once seen as an unexciting destination, Brisbane's appeal has increased over the years and it is evolving into a viable alternative to Sydney or Melbourne as an expat base.

Laid-back and offering the buzz of a big city without the logistical challenges, Brisbane is making great strides towards becoming a cosmopolitan centre. Modern and clean, Brisbane has a thriving café culture, a growing number and range of excellent eateries, a compact CBD, and sprawling suburbs. In terms of affordability, Brisbane is attractive, with like-for-like houses at prices generally lower than in Sydney and Melbourne.

Either side of Brisbane, along the coast, you have the Sunshine Coast (north) and the Gold Coast (south). These are popular tourist spots offering amusement and theme parks, water parks, and the famous Australia Zoo. Heading north, you have foodie haven, Noosa; Hervey Bay; and the heritage listed Fraser Island, stretching a little farther up to the bottom tip of the Great Barrier Reef and the Whitsundays – a most beautiful and breathtaking part of Australia and, indeed, the world. The famous, swirling Whitehaven Beach can be found around about here. Farther up the coast you will reach Cairns (1,704km north of Brisbane), a common spot for tourists wishing to experience the Great Barrier Reef. The not very originally named Far North Queensland is home to tropical and lush, agricultural land, where sugar cane and tropical fruits are grown, and is also a popular tourist destination, with Port Douglas the main centre.

FLIGHT TIMES TO MAJOR CITIES FROM BRISBANE AIRPORT

Adelaide: 2 hours
Melbourne: 1.5 hours
Perth: 5 hours
Sydney: 1.5 hours

CLIMATE AND GEOGRAPHY

Queensland's size results in varied weather around the state: tropical and monsoonal in the Far North, near the equator, and generally humid, warm weather most of the year along the coast. Summers can be wet and winters can be cool, but the temperature variance is typically lower in the north compared to the likes of NSW and VIC. In reality, Queensland experiences two seasons – warm and not so warm! Inland and less populated areas tend to experience lower temperatures overall.

Queensland is home to the largest area of agricultural land in Australia. From livestock to tropical fruit, there is a thriving agricultural economy. Mining is another prominent industry, and other business investment is starting to follow the skills and population growth the state is experiencing.

SOUTH AUSTRALIA (SA) - ADELAIDE

South Australia is positioned in the middle south part of the country and is most recognised for the famous Barossa wine region. Its capital, Adelaide, is on the south coast of the state. Farther north is the hostile but beautiful Outback region of Uluru (Ayers Rock) and Alice Springs in the Northern Territory, near enough in the centre of Australia. With a population of just over 1.5 million, SA is home to the smallest population of the five mainland states. The majority of the population reside in the Adelaide region, with the remainder close by in the region lining the coast.

Adelaide is known as the 'City of Churches'. The main CBD is fairly compact and well laid out, with wide streets that are easy to navigate. Adelaide hosts a number of festivals and events, with a lively food and wine scene. Located amongst some of Australia's best-known wine regions, Adelaide has a down-to-earth vibe. The Barossa Valley, Clare Valley, Adelaide Hills, and McLaren Vale produce a great selection of wines sold all around the world and are home to many of the larger of Australian wine producers that you commonly see in the UK.

FLIGHT TIMES TO MAJOR CITIES FROM ADELAIDE AIRPORT

Brisbane: 1.5 hours

Melbourne: 1 hour
Perth: 5 hours
Sydney: 2 hours

CLIMATE AND GEOGRAPHY

The vast inland area of SA experiences hot and dry weather, especially during the summer. In the more heavily populated area of Adelaide and surrounds near the coast, the weather is sunny and hot during summer, cooler in spring and autumn, and mild and rainy through winter. There are elevated areas to the North of Adelaide which experience a cooler climate, perfect for producing cooler-climate wines in the Adelaide Hills region.

TASMANIA (TAS) - HOBART

Tasmania is a beautiful island state in the south eastern part of Australia, separated from the mainland by the Bass Strait. The mention of 'Tassie' conjures up images of the Tasmanian devil, as well as of the magnificent Wineglass Bay. Melbourne is the closest mainland city and offers ferries to Tasmania. The population of Tasmania is just over 500,000, half of whom reside in the state's capital of Hobart in the south. Launceston is the other large city, located in the north. Tasmania has a great reputation for quality produce and wine and has a great food scene. The climate is cooler than the rest of Australia; with four distinct seasons and a higher rainfall than the rest of the country, it is often described as similar to the UK climate.

VICTORIA (VIC) - MELBOURNE

Victoria is the most densely populated state in Australia and second to NSW in terms of overall population count, with almost 6 million people. Of this, the majority, roughly 4 million, reside in the Greater Melbourne area. Victoria is the smallest mainland state, positioned in the south eastern pocket of the country, with Melbourne perched at the top of Port Phillip Bay.

Not many people know what to expect of Melbourne, the state's capital. Whilst perhaps not as obviously beautiful as Sydney, Melbourne offers a European feel. The Yarra River runs through the CBD, with the casino a major landmark on the South Bank. The main CBD area is home to many fantastic restaurants and the famous Melbourne laneways, offering cafés and restaurants in an intimate street-side setting. The culinary scene is sophisticated in Melbourne; many acclaimed restaurants are based here, and Melbournians are proud of their gastronomic prowess.

Melbourne is home to many Greek and Italian migrants, resulting in more of a European feel than any other of the state capitals. Within a few hours of Melbourne you will find two major wine regions in the Yarra Valley, to the north, and the Mornington Peninsula, to the south east. The Great Ocean Road, to the west of Melbourne, is home to the famous 12 Apostles and a thriving tourist stretch running from Torquay through to Warnambool.

FLIGHT TIMES TO MAJOR CITIES FROM MELBOURNE TULLAMARINE AIRPORT

Adelaide: 1.5 hours
Brisbane: 2 hours

Perth: 4 hours

Sydney: 1 hour

Melbourne has a second airport, Melbourne Avalon, serving domestic flights – most typically low-cost airlines.

CLIMATE AND GEOGRAPHY

Victoria has a variable climate and is the mainland's wettest state. The saying goes that if you don't like the weather in Melbourne, just wait ten minutes – it will likely change. It's entirely feasible that you'll experience 'four seasons in one day' when in Melbourne. Overall, summers are warm, with temperatures regularly hitting 30–35°C, spring and autumn are mild, and winter can be cold and crisp, with a common range of 5–10°C. Melbourne is the only city where you'll occasionally find central heating – an odd sight here in Australia.

The Alpine and Grampian mountain ranges in northern parts of Victoria are elevated enough to allow for skiing in the winter. Northern Victoria, bordering NSW, is also home to the Goulbourn Murray Irrigation District, a large, agricultural area affectionately named 'Victoria's Food Bowl'.

WESTERN AUSTRALIA (WA) - PERTH

Located across the entire western part of the country, Western Australia is the largest state in Australia. WA attracts the second largest number of UK migrants after NSW. With a population of 2.5 million, the majority of people live in the south-west corner of the state, where its capital city, Perth, is located. Perth is closer to parts of Indonesia than some of Australia and is very isolated, with the closest Australian city being Adelaide, over 2,000 kilometres away. This is similar to the distance from London to Madrid or Bucharest! The distances are considerable in WA, often with long stretches of road and not much else. WA's economy is largely dominated by the mining industry, with iron ore the state's largest export.

The state's capital, Perth, is set on the Swan River, with the city's greater region home to nearly 2 million people. A compact city, Perth is easy to navigate and has become home to an increasing number of restaurants and cafés to support the growing population. Perth tends to be bustling during the day, but can be said to have a quieter nightlife. Many of Perth's residential areas stretch north and south of the city, popular with families desiring a more laid-back lifestyle. A large house with a pool and close proximity to the beach is not uncommon here, although popularity has driven property prices up considerably over the past 10–15 years.

The famous port of Fremantle is located to the south of the city and is a quaint town, home to a widely known and loved market, alfresco dining, boutique breweries, and fish restaurants. With a vibrant music scene, Fremantle pubs and bars attract many from the city. Drive farther south, to the west, and you will find the boutique wine and gourmet region of Margaret River, whilst passing beaches, farmland, and forest. A long drive north of Perth will land you in the Coral Coast region, with its lesser known heritage-listed reef, Ningaloo, where you can swim with whale sharks and other marine life. To the far north of WA, you will find Broome and the famous Kimberley region, with its Bungle Bungle range – characterised by red, rocky terrain, hills, and canyons.

FLIGHT TIMES TO MAJOR CITIES FROM PERTH AIRPORT

Adelaide: 3 hours

Brisbane: 5 hours

Melbourne: 4 hours

Sydney: 5 hours

CLIMATE AND GEOGRAPHY

WA is a very large state and the climate of the coastal and populated areas varies greatly from the inland desert and bush region. Perth is known for being sunnier than any other capital city and experiences dry weather most of the year around. Summers are hot, with warm balmy evenings; winters are cooler and wetter. Inland WA experiences hotter, more desert-like weather. The north is tropical and humid.

Facts in this section sourced from www.australia.gov.au

Still, why Australia?

A relatively young country with a small population, Australia is full of opportunity and growth. The thriving economy and the country's resources offer a broad range of employment options and business opportunities. Its efficient infrastructure, modern and tolerant society, and relaxed lifestyle provide a high standard and quality of living.

The proximity to a corner of the world unreached by many gives Australia a mystical air. Many countries such as Indonesia, New Zealand, and the Pacific Islands are in fact closer to Australian land than some parts of Australia itself. The opportunity to be placed in this part of the world for at least some of your life can provide another world of travel and experiences. Asia, especially, is, for all intents and purposes, a similar proposition to Continental Europe from the UK, albeit on a much larger scale, offering a different stimulation for your senses. Exploring the Orient and South East Asia is fun and enriching – what an exciting prospect to have this within reach geographically. Australia itself is so enchanting, from snorkelling in the Great Barrier Reef, to trekking The Kimberley, or exploring the wine regions, and you will experience much that is not possible anywhere else on this planet.

Considered by some Brits to be a 'hotter Britain', it surprises many that, culturally speaking, Australia is subtly very different to the UK. The cultural diversity of Australia's population offers great access to wonderful cuisines and cultural insights. You will meet people from all corners of the world, and, once accustomed to this, you won't bat an eyelid when someone tells you they've come from Outer Mongolia or Timbuktu to study or work. Similarly, you can experience food from any cuisine and annual festivals celebrating every conceivable culture and nationality.

A FEW FACTS

- ▶ Average income is $73,000 per annum*
- ▶ Unemployment rate as at September 2013 is 5.7%*
- ▶ Current Government is the Liberal Party of Australia, with Tony Abbott as Prime Minister
- ▶ Population as at March 2013 is 23 million*
- ▶ 26% of Australia's population was born overseas^

- 20% of the population has at least one overseas-born parent^

- Median sale prices, houses, AU$ as at June 2013:**

    ▽ Adelaide $435,153

    ▽ Brisbane $440,454

    ▽ Melbourne $553,447

    ▽ Perth $584,487

    ▽ Sydney $690,064

- Median sale prices, units (apartments), AU$ as at June 2013:**

    ▽ Adelaide $280,219

    ▽ Brisbane $346,964

    ▽ Melbourne $411,714

    ▽ Perth $386,798

    ▽ Sydney $491,845

*Australian Bureau of Statistics (ABS)
**www.domain.com.au
^2011 Census

UK migrants to Australia

According to the Australian Department of Immigration and Border Protection and the 2011 Census:

- In 2011–12, more than 54,000 people from the UK moved to Australia. Of those, 26,161 were permanent arrivals, and 28,730 were issued a business (subclass 457) visa for a stay of up to 4 years.

- In the same period, 6,896 permanent residents who originated from the UK decided to leave, of whom 57% returned to the UK

- 25% of UK-born residents chose to reside in NSW; 21% chose WA.

- WA attracted 31% of skilled migrants in 2011–12, and NSW 26%.

Culture the Aussie way

Australia's culture is essentially 'Western', borne out of its unique history of the convict, working and sporting heroes, and its earliest colonialists. The philosophy of 'mateship' and a 'fair go' are key principles of Aussie culture, with a sense of ensuring justice for battlers and the underdog. Respect, equality, and freedom are at the core of Aussie values, along with tolerance for diversity, given its long history of migration.

Fiercely patriotic, the deep sense of Australian pride is most obviously exhibited around sporting occasions. For the most part, Australians are sports mad. Rugby, cricket, tennis, swimming, soccer (English football), AFL (Australian Rules football) – whatever the sporting occasion, you can be sure it will be a topic of anticipation over the weekend and of conversation in the Monday morning coffee queue. Patriotism is also evident in a lot of marketing and advertising, and Aussies will often favour products, produce, or companies that are Australian made or born.

Aussies tend to be direct (some would say blunt). Their appreciation for honesty drives a tendency to say exactly what they think, without mincing words. This came as a huge shock to me, more used to the English propensity to beat around the bush so as not to offend! Bluntness, on the border of rudeness, can characterise many a customer-service experience, which can be a source of frustration and bewilderment upon arrival. This is improving, but old habits die hard and it's all part of the 'charm' and experience. Sense of humour is a common bonding approach and it is generally a good sign in terms of social acceptance. The Australian sense of humour can sometimes be perceived as macho, blokey, and even sexist. This is a topical discussion point, given a 2013 Ernst & Young report declaring Australian businesses as sexist; citing macho culture as a reason for low numbers of female leaders in business.

The Australian lifestyle is, overall, very relaxed and laid back. The Australian dream is quality of life that involves owning property, signifying independence and autonomy. With the vast majority of the population in Australia living a short distance from the coast, the beach and BBQ lifestyle is desired, achievable, and enjoyed by most.

SO, YOU'RE A POM? EXPAT LIFE IN AUSTRALIA

Being an expat anywhere is exciting and can be exhilarating. You are part of a special club that only a few will dare venture into. According to www.feedbacq.com, expats make up 3.1% of the global population. You will not feel out of place as a Brit (POM) in Australia, however, make sure you remember that you are taking a bold step – one that you should consider a great achievement. This is before you even land Down Under.

As a POM in Australia, you will be welcomed and won't feel out of place. According to the Australian Bureau of Statistics (ABS), the UK was the largest source of migrants to Australia in 2010, with 14.5% of all migrants coming from the UK. Except for the teasing about being a POM and the sporting rivalry, you will be warmly welcomed and will immediately have a sense that you can expect a straightforward integration.

According to HSBC's 2012 Explorer Survey, Australia has been voted the top destination for the promise of a better quality of life. 77% said they can integrate well, compared to a global average of 58%, and more than half, 52%, agree it's an easy place to make friends, versus a global average of 44%. So you aren't alone in thinking that Australia is a great choice of country in which to spend at least a portion of your life.

Having said all of this, setting realistic and informed expectations is crucial to whether you will consider your move to Australia a success. A successful relocation will depend on a huge number of factors, many of which may be out of your control. One of these factors is your ability to cope with the related emotions and adapt to the change that you have made to your life. Anyone with the financial means to make this move can fill in the forms and go through the motions. But it's patience, positivity, persistence, and other personal attributes which will determine whether you thrive and enjoy your new home.

The truth is that expat life, and, indeed, being an expat in Australia, is not for everyone. Britons returning to the UK after failing to settle are often referred to as 'Ping Pong Poms' or 'Boomerang POMs'. Research has shown that up to one third of Britons decide to give up on Australia and return to the UK. The reality is that some arrive with the promise of a new life and fresh opportunities, only to find that they cannot overcome the homesickness, to discover that the distance is insurmountable, or that they have not sufficiently managed the financial side of the move. Other reasons cited for a returning to the UK are the high cost of living, the inability to feel 'at home', boredom, being too far away... the list goes on. Life here is not for everyone, and there are so many variables to whether your relocation will be a success. Another truth which many people do not consider is the impact of a transient population. These Ping Pong Poms may be your close friends. Expat assignments end, and people decide to move on. This is a sad fact of life, and friendship circles here can be ever evolving. Some may dwindle altogether.

Being an eternal expat, I thought that my move to Sydney would be a proverbial walk in the park. It was my eighteenth international move. All of my lessons had been learnt, surely? I lived in Egypt at the height of the '80s terror frenzy; moved to Germany without speaking so much as a word of German; moved to the US with a suitcase and no expectations. I have never been as wrong as I was when I thought moving to Australia would be easy. I made many mistakes and had a list as long as my arm of misconceptions and wrongly held beliefs of what my life here would be like, and what I could expect. Believing it would be easy and not appreciating the cultural differences were two huge mistakes, which cost me my happiness for my first years here. Yes, years. Needless to say, I love my life now. I've worked hard to make a real go of it and have come out the other side happier for it. I wouldn't live anywhere else. But a word of caution - you really do need to invest time into adjusting, making new friends, and learning what to expect.

As with any process we embark on, there will be expectations and what we think is adequate preparation. Whilst the old adage 'learn from your mistakes' is apt here, it's best to avoid making too many mistakes, as this serves to decrease your morale and confidence. As much as possible, it's good to know that you're not alone in this, and to know what types of mistakes and misconceptions are commonly made. Try to avoid them, or at least be on the alert for them.

Five common mistakes

1. Not enough research, or not knowing what to expect - the more research you do, the more familiar everything will become. Knowing what to expect will help to minimise a constant state of anticipation in your early days. This state of being is exhausting and frustrating. Look into areas, schools, and what your lifestyle could be like. I hope this book will help bridge your knowledge gaps so that you have at least a rough idea of what's coming your way and can make more informed decisions.

2. Not asking for help – whether it's asking for help from loved ones or those you're moving with, make sure you do ask. Many also make the mistake of thinking that navigating the visa system or customs is straightforward or dismiss professional advice, thinking it's possible to go it alone. Understandably, you may be put off by seemingly high fees and feel the money is better spent elsewhere. I agree this may be the case, depending on your budget and level of confidence in handling some issues. However, there is no harm in asking for advice or shopping around for quotes. You can then weigh up whether it's more cost and time effective to enlist a professional versus the stress and burden of

doing it yourself. Not to mention the risk, possible consequences, and additional costs if you make a mistake, miss a deadline, or get the wrong advice – these may be considerably more costly in the end.

3. Underestimating costs – of living and of moving. Again, this comes down to research and ensuring you have a contingency fund. Typically, things are always more than expected, and processes tend to take longer than we anticipate. I'm not sure of the science behind this one, but don't you find this to be the case? Moving is a costly process – there is more on this, and what to expect, in the coming sections. Australia is expensive, your salary will likely differ to that in the UK, and, income tax here is higher. Throw these into the mix, and, at the very least, draft a spreadsheet of the items you typically spend money on in a month; research the similar cost levels in Australia. Inevitably, you will be much more aware of your outgoings in a new environment when you are likely on a stricter budget before your first salary payment. It pays to do this exercise to minimise any surprises on all counts.

4. Moving money with a bank rather than a broker – if you are moving more than a few hundred £ Sterling, you should have at least a phone call with a currency broker. They specialise in currency and their services are often much cheaper than traditional bank transfers. This call will almost certainly save you money.

5. Not making the effort to network and meet people – there is a common preconception that everyone in Australia is friendly and outgoing, leading to the expectation that making friends will be easy. Whilst it is not impossible, forging new friendships is challenging. Achieving the depth of familiarity that you have with

friends you've known for years takes time and patience. When you are lonely and feeling isolated, it is easy to forget this. It will take time, lots of effort, accepting every invitation, and being open. On the plus side, I found it so much easier to connect with new people here than in the UK – especially fellow Brits. The simple fact that you are both in Australia and have made the same choice quickly helps to forge a common bond. Sign up for exercise classes, find a sports team, go for after-work drinks, join a networking or 'meet up' group, ensure that any friends or acquaintances introduce you to anyone they know in Australia. While it might be stepping outside your comfort zone, it is necessary to help establish a network of friends, which is an essential part of settling in.

Seven common misconceptions

1. The culture is broadly the same – as will become clearer during the course of this book, Aussie culture is very different to British culture. There are similarities, of course, but you won't be alone in thinking that the differences are quite stark once you scratch the surface.

2. It'll be easy – moving is a challenging process. Relocating to Australia involves a great distance, complex logistics, and effort to ensure it goes smoothly. It's an exciting process, but to believe that it's as simple as packing up and flying out is somewhat naïve – there is a lot of work involved in a smooth move.

3. It's like being on holiday – many, including myself, were fooled into thinking that life in Australia would be like being on a permanent holiday. The surroundings are beautiful, and sometimes you will

pinch yourself to believe that you are really here, but the washing and chores still need to be done, you will be working, and you will want to slump on the couch after a busy week rather than be on the go and exploring like a tourist.

4. Everyone lives by the beach – 80% of the population live within driving distance of the coastline, so it's easy to believe the images of properties and life on the water. Whilst achievable, living by the water is not always realistic, or, indeed, desired by everyone. There are plenty of beautiful suburbs to choose from in any city, and where you choose to live will depend on your budget and circumstances.

5. No doubt about it, Australia is full of Australians! I'll have loads of Aussie friends – I assumed that I'd meet many more Australians than I have done in my time here. The truth is that there are so many fellow expats that you will gravitate to, by virtue of the very big thing you have in common that bonds you. Many expats find that meeting people is a challenge and inevitably click with others in the same position. You don't have to move far or be too alert to hear the familiar English accent – which is always comforting, no matter how adventurous you intend to be on your stay here.

6. BBQ and knock-off-early Fridays – the working culture came as a cold, hard shock to me. Like most people, I believed that the working week was very relaxed and never imagined that Aussies worked some of the longest hours in the world. This is partially due to our inability these days to switch off, with smartphones and constantly being connected. However, surveys show that many Aussies work more than the standard 35–40 hour week.

According to the Organisation for Economic Co-operation and Development's Better Life Index, 14% of Australian workers put in more than 50 hours per week. In short, it's best not to expect an 'easy life' at work, and, whilst a Friday BBQ on the office roof terrace is not unusual, it's certainly not the norm.

7. It doesn't get cold – Australia does have a winter in most populated regions. Of course, it is known to get very hot, and images of the red outback, beaches, and tropics give the impression of perennial heat and summer. Melbourne and Sydney, especially, do experience a winter season. Elevated areas, such as the Blue Mountains region and the Victoria Alpine regions, commonly get snow in the winter. Every winter, there is a thriving, albeit short, ski season in the likes of the Snowy and Alpine Mountain ranges.

Your foray into expat life

Settling into expat life is a process. There is the physical relocation, the hoops to jump through as you register and comply with the relevant authorities, the establishing of a new home and lifestyle – all whilst navigating a new environment. It is important to have a routine and to determine what will help create a sense of normality, gently balanced with maximising the experience of your new home.

If you are looking for a job, it's worth allocating a time every day to deal with applications, phone calls, and, of course, interviews. It may feel like you have to be 'on the case' every waking hour until you find a job. This is the one mistake almost everyone makes – to lock themselves away on the job hunt, too guilty to enjoy any free time. When they do find a job, there is little time to explore the city and it takes longer to acclimatise. Not to mention the exhaustion that results from being in a new place and constantly on guard for a phone call about your job prospects. The same applies if you have come over with a job. Try to spend some fun time exploring and doing some of the 'touristy' bits before getting into the daily commitment of work.

The challenge in the first few weeks and months of moving is the range of emotions you will feel. Isolation, a sense that you stand out or don't fit in, homesickness, stress, loneliness, and frustration are all normal. There is also a perpetual anticipation of the unknown. You will experience a natural tendency to compare everything to the UK and find a 'like for like'. Comparing currency back to £ Sterling will also be normal. This helps to build your knowledge and provides a point of reference. However, it's best to start thinking 'local' as soon as possible, given you'll be earning Australian Dollars, and comparisons should be in relation to your disposable income rather than £ Sterling, which relates to your UK income.

The fear and sense of limbo is something that should be addressed here. You will likely feel both at some stage, and it may be hard to stop yourself from booking the next flight home. The simplest of tasks will seem so difficult, and the grass will appear much greener – you will wonder why on earth you decided to move in the first place.

Have a plan on how you will cope with wobbly days – such as having a wish-list of things you want to do when in Australia. An ideal time to take time out to do something fun is when you're feeling a bit low. The distraction will help, and seeing something new will remind you of the reasons you moved here in the first place. Visiting a museum, going to a beach, taking a trip to a wine region, simply enjoying the city like a tourist – whatever it is, always have a back-up activity to keep you busy. It's an amazing and strange dichotomy – feeling everything around you is new, but at the same time realising that this is where you are building your home! Routine is also key, and I will touch on this again in later sections.

STEP 1

SIZE UP

The prospect of moving to a new country can be exciting and daunting in equal measure. Australia has the benefit of being English speaking with a seemingly similar culture to the UK, but the distance is a huge drawback. Will this hold you back from the opportunity of a lifetime?

Of course, you must weigh up the pros and cons before making any large change to your life. Here are some of the key considerations when deciding if this move is for you:

A matter of time

Timing is everything. If you decide to embark on this adventure, you will need to consider the planning time you have available. This will be determined by visa processing periods, your job offer, personal circumstances such as children and/or pets, ensuring you have the savings necessary – or all of the above. If you are relocating with your job, it may be a matter of weeks before you can set sail – in which case, there is much to do in a very short time. If you are planning to make a more permanent move, your visa may take 12–24 months, and you may need this length of time, or longer, to obtain the visa and financial security necessary to make the leap.

Distance matters

Australia is a large country, and a flight from the west (e.g. Perth) to east (e.g. Sydney) coast will take five hours. Flights between the other capitals can take one to three hours, with the Adelaide–Melbourne leg being the shortest and Sydney–Melbourne the most travelled. Driving long distances within Australia is common, with many who wouldn't flinch at driving eight to ten hours straight from Sydney to Melbourne, for example.

Average holiday accommodation and travelling in Australia can be costly due to high labour rates, and the recent high Australian Dollar has encouraged travel on a global scale. Consider that the shortest international flight from most capital cities will be at least three hours. Popular destinations such as Bali and Thailand are a seven to nine hour flight away; Fiji and the Pacific Islands are a three to five hour journey.

It is quite common for Aussies to save up their leave for longer holidays to account for the distance they need to travel to get anywhere.

Of course, you will be considering the trip back to the UK to visit family and friends. If you're lucky enough, they may also have the means and enthusiasm to pay you a visit to share your experience in Australia. The distance can't be ignored – the prospect of 24 hours of travelling is daunting and gruelling. Managing jet lag and other effects of the long journey can also add to the stress of what should be a fun trip. Returning with children, especially, can challenge the most patient of individuals.

Having said all of that, there are tens of flights per day to the UK from most cities in Australia. The 24-hour journey between Australia and the UK is affectionately called the 'Kangaroo Route'. In the whole scheme of things, the cost is good value considering the distance. Airlines have picked up their game significantly over the years (mostly due to the stiff and unforgiving level of competition on this route), and the experience can be quite comfortable with patience and the right frame of mind. You can soften the effects of the long journey by having stopovers in fantastic cities like Singapore, Dubai, or Bangkok. This all adds to the fun and adventure of a life Down Under.

Family, friends, and pets

Undoubtedly, family and friends are priorities when considering any move. Your partner and children, if any, will likely be your first consideration. This will be followed swiftly by thoughts of who you will be leaving behind. Whilst it may not be a top consideration, you must also think about the opportunity to meet new people and the friendships you might forge in your Australian life.

YOUR IMMEDIATE FAMILY

A trailing spouse/partner buy-in is crucial to the success of the move. Most relocations fail because of a partner's inability to settle and feel at home. According to corporate mobility surveys, two thirds of expat spouses have careers in their home country and do not work when on their partner's international assignment. Whilst their working partner has a routine and is occupied during the week, the trailing spouse may harbour resentment due to boredom, loneliness, and putting their own career on hold.

If you are moving with children, it is important to consider their age, education stage, and, of course, their personality. Whilst difficult to predict how such a move will impact on a child, it is key that the transition is managed with sensitivity, especially considering their age and vulnerabilities associated with 'fitting in' at a new school and with a new social circle.

In general terms, Australia is a relaxed and friendly place. The culture and environment tend to encourage tolerance, respect, and independence. The lifestyle is very sociable and is there for the taking. It is key to communicate, have a positive frame of mind, and understand everyone's expectations, concerns, and what they hope to get from their time in Australia.

On the flipside, repatriation back to the UK for all involved can, in some cases, be more challenging than the move abroad. The sense of novelty and the excitement of being in a new environment can be addictive. The prospect of returning 'home' and to the 'normality' of a previous lifestyle can be scary and life-changing. It's entirely possible that you'll feel destined for a more permanent stay abroad – be prepared!

My own experience is a case in point here. I have a younger brother who was exposed to the exact same childhood as I. By the time we went to university, we had both lived in more than ten countries and had attended as many schools (some for as little as three months, and in developing countries). These circumstances were far from ideal and certainly not 'normal'! I seemed to thrive on the ability to make a fresh start, was able to adapt quickly to my surroundings, made friends quickly, and developed a staunch exterior to cope with whatever challenges each transition would bring. I have continued in my father's footsteps and have spent most of my adulthood as an expat. I relish the opportunity to push myself outside of my comfort zone, and the fact that I am living on the other side of the planet from my family isn't front of mind. I live by the same philosophy as Lucille Ball, who once said, "I'd rather regret the things I've done than regret the things I haven't done."

Like chalk to cheese, my brother's destiny and desires have been the polar opposite. Much more conservative, devoid of any travel bug, my brother lives five minutes from my parents in England and is happy doing so. We truly challenge the nature vs. nurture theories!

FAMILY AND FRIENDS YOU LEAVE BEHIND

There will be a 24-hour flight and jet lag standing in between you and the people you most care about. This will be considered simple logistics for some and the worst possible scenario for others. Deciding where you are on the scale is an important factor. Think about the length of your intended stay, propensity for both you and your loved ones to make the trip, and how often you'll want to make it. Will your financial situation allow for regular trips? Fortunately, in this age of Skype and other social media, the world has never felt smaller.

There is a great opportunity for the whole family to explore and travel together – joint holidays and meeting in different countries so that everyone gets a holiday can be memorable and a great experience for all involved. On any given day, there are almost thirty flights departing from Sydney to Europe via Asia – competition is fierce and fares relatively affordable. The world is literally your oyster.

Be prepared for the guilt that will set in – possibly even a feeling of selfishness that you've upset the family and circle of friends somewhat and have made things awkward for everyone to satisfy your own goals and needs. For me, this happened well before I left, to the extent that I considered whether I should leave at all. For many, it might not happen until months or years after arrival, once the excitement wears off. Replacing life-long friends and the security of established relationships will be impossible in the short term. Not having your nearest and dearest at the end of the phone in the same time zone or only a car ride away will make you feel lonely and isolated. This is a horrible feeling that you need to be prepared for. There is no simple answer or approach for this one. You have to be prepared to make bucket loads of effort, and, even if you don't feel like it, to accept every invitation that you receive. All of them – even if you don't understand AFL and have been invited to a game, or will feel awkward turning up to a BBQ or party on your own. You must do it – you'll be surprised at who you meet, the connections you'll make, and how friendly people will be, knowing that you're new to Australia. At the very least, you can ask burning questions or get a hint or two about life here. Be prepared to join networking or other groups that share similar interests. There will be expat groups, sports clubs/teams, yoga groups, gyms, and many other groups that share similar interests to you. If you have children, get involved with school activities; go to the sports matches and fetes. Whether it's a cooking class, hiking tour, or becoming involved at the local church, it's crucial to get stuck in no matter how far out of your comfort zone you might feel.

Whilst making friends in Australia is tough, there is a certain camaraderie that comes from meeting fellow Brits and other expats. I mistakenly thought that moving here permanently would somehow result in lots of Aussie friends and all would be well. For the first few years, at least, I couldn't count a single Aussie amongst my friends. Brits, Germans, Dutch, Americans, but not one Aussie! What I found was that many Australians of my age were very much in school and university friendship groups. I suppose this isn't unlike it is in the UK – once there is a circle of friends, the demands on your time will likely mean you have a hard enough time catching up with your established circle, let alone bringing new friendships into the mix.

Start preparing for this before you leave. Where possible, seek out opportunities to connect with people in advance. If you're looking for a job, join networking groups using social media such as LinkedIn and get some conversations started. Play an instrument? Track down a band. If you play football or tennis, make enquiries about teams and matches.

PETS

There are an estimated 33 million pets in Australia – the population of pets is much larger than the human population. The catch, though, is that there is fierce protection of Australian borders and traffic in and out. Animals are not exempt from the strict customs and import laws in Australia. At time of writing, pets from the

UK will be held for a minimum of ten days in quarantine, a recent reduction from 30 days and a welcome change to the regulations for pets from designated countries. This follows a number of blood tests, permission to import, and meeting a host of criteria and requirements to ensure compliance. More on this in Step 2.

Consider using a transport agent to assist with such a complex process. This will add to your relocation budget, but I'm certain it is worth saving the stress of doing it yourself.

Fear of missing out (FOMO)

Weddings, births, deaths, Christmases, birthdays, anniversaries, celebrations, reunions: life will continue without you, and, at the same time, you and your family will be creating memories in Australia that cannot be shared first-hand with family and friends in the UK.

This can be isolating and potentially upsetting, testing your ability to let go and your determination to integrate into Aussie life.

It's worth considering how you will deal with this; be prepared to come to terms with it.

Immigration status and qualifications

It's no secret that Australia has relied heavily on migration to fulfil skills shortages and help with economic growth. At the time of writing, skills in demand range from engineers, doctors, and tradespeople, through to boat builders.

Immigration rules, requirements, and policies are very complex and constantly changing. In fact, they are usually out of date as soon as they are printed! To find out the latest information, visit the Australian Government website: www.immi.gov.au.

Either you or an agent can then determine the best visa for your circumstances. To find a registered migration agent, visit www.mara.gov.au.

In very simple terms, a skilled professional has two options to reside and work in Australia. If you are lucky enough to have family ties in Australia, you may be eligible to apply for residency this way (subject to certain criteria).

PERMANENT RESIDENCY (PR)

In broad terms, to apply for permanent residency, you must have either certain skills in demand or a relationship with an Australian PR or citizen (i.e. you are engaged to be married, are a de facto spouse, or have family ties to Australia).

Proof of relationships and/or skills involves a lengthy process, lots of documentation, and form filling. For the skilled stream, you need to qualify for as many points as possible in support of your application. Varying points are given based on age, English language ability, skills (both for you and your spouse), qualifications, and so on. This is not for the faint-hearted (taking usually no less than one year and most likely closer to two years).

The process involves providing in-depth proof of your skills to ensure you meet a demand. Be prepared for plenty of paperwork gathering, a CV overhaul, references, proof of spousal relationship (if any), and long waits during the process. Note that you must have a medical with a registered doctor (including a chest x-ray to test for tuberculosis and an HIV test if over the age of 15 years) and declare any existing medical concerns. You will also be subject to police clearance checks from any country you have lived in for more than 12 months over the past 10 years since you turned 16 years of age.

Navigating this process is fraught with anxiety and wonder – and, again, is not immune to change. The general danger zone for amendments tends to be the start of a new financial year – which in Australia runs from 1st July–30th June. However, changes can, and will, happen at any time.

My journey to Australian residency took 18 months from the initial meeting with a migration agent to having the visas stamped in our passports. The painful process of proving my husband's skills alone took half that time. He works in IT and at that time was a contractor, with assignments ranging from weeks to months. Contacting all his previous managers to vouch for his skills and expanding his CV to six pages was arduous to say the least. Once all of his skills were documented and verified, we had to wait for the rubber stamp to say that these skills matched the requirements, and we duly received the bulk of our points to continue with the process to lodge the actual visa application.

While gathering final paperwork, and just days away from our final lodgement, we received news that the points required for our application had increased. In an instant, we were five points short of the required number of points and our dream was seemingly in tatters. We were devastated. In consultation with our migration agent, we had only one option to top up the points: come up with

AU$20,000 to invest in government bonds, refundable a year after settling in Australia. We begged, borrowed, and stole (ok, not quite!) to get the funds together – if it were not for the support of our family, our life would have turned out very differently.

Arriving in Australia as a PR means:

▶ You are not restricted to one employer.

▶ That, after a waiting period, you can apply to become a citizen (dual-citizenship is permitted for both Australians and Britons).

▶ Children can access the public schooling system without additional fees.

▶ You can purchase property and are entitled to any governments grants and rebates, if applicable.

TEMPORARY WORK SKILLED (457) VISA

The alternate option is employer sponsorship. This gives the right to temporary residency within Australia. The process is generally straightforward, although it has recently become more stringent. Employers must prove that they have looked to the Australian labour market to fulfil their skill needs. This will generally take a few weeks, dependent on whether there are any hold ups in the system, or if you need to supply further information in support of your application.

Those relocating with a company will most likely be sponsored for this visa. The 457 visa applicant can apply to have their family and/or spouse registered on the same visa. This permits the spouse to work whilst in Australia.

Some brave souls may choose to come over on a tourist (at the time of writing this is called an eVisitor visa) or working holiday visa (if under the age of 31 years). As a British citizen, you can apply for the electronic authority to visit Australia for either tourism or business purposes. If you choose 'business' as your sole purpose for visiting, this permits you to seek business and employment opportunities during a maximum three-month stay – however, you are not allowed to earn an income on this visa. Depending on your skills and the market at the time, you may be fortunate to find an employer willing to sponsor you to stay on a 457 visa. Those young enough for a working holiday visa must meet certain requirements to work whilst travelling and, again, may wish to stay longer with employer sponsorship. These and other immigration laws are subject to constant change, so a visit to www.immi.gov.au is strongly advised.

In general, those applying for a 457 visa will not be required to have a medical. There are exceptions, however, such as those choosing to practice medicine or work in a hospital or childcare facility. You may also be asked to provide police clearance checks.

Being a sponsored Temporary Resident means:

- ▶ You are restricted to the employer sponsoring you, and your residency is dependent on employment.

- ▶ After a period (at time of writing, two years), the employer can sponsor you for PR.

- ▶ Depending on your home state, public schooling may need to be paid for as an overseas student (at time of writing, some states are reviewing this policy: refer to the Education Board for the relevant state).

- Buying a property is more complex as it must be approved by a foreign investment board.
- Welfare and social security are not accessible.

ARE YOUR SKILLS RECOGNISED IN AUSTRALIA?

Depending on your profession, you may need recognition/verification of your qualifications to work in Australia, or you may need to obtain local qualifications or certifications before you may work in your chosen field. This can apply to a range of professions, ranging from doctors, nurses, insurance experts, lawyers... It is crucial that you check this with the Australian government to know in advance how your skills will be recognised (or not) in Australia. Check via this section of their website: www.immi.gov.au/asri.

Medical matters

There is a reciprocal agreement between the UK and Australia allowing Brits temporarily in Australia to access the government's Medicare system. This is a subsidised system where you may incur out-of-pocket expenses for medical treatment. Even optional health insurance does not secure fee-free medical treatment, as doctors and hospitals often charge more than the rebate amount. This will leave you with what is called a 'gap' to pay.

In general, the health system in Australia is sophisticated, efficient, and offers a great standard of care. This shouldn't be a topic for concern, outside of the fact that you may have out-of-pocket expenses as it is not free like the NHS.

Money matters

Money and finances feature high on the checklist of considerations when making any trip abroad. A clear overview and financial plan are essential to a successful move. There will inevitably be a period where you may not be drawing an income, so it is crucial to plan for this and have access to sufficient funds to see you through your first few weeks or months in Australia. Allow for an adjustment period when you familiarise yourself with the new currency and cost of living. It is also worth factoring in a buffer or emergency fund for any unexpected occurrences.

If moving with an employer, you must consider the package on offer not just against your current arrangements and market value, but also in line with the cost of living in Australia.

Consider some or all of the following when thinking about your financial situation:

- ▶ How much will the move cost?

- ▶ What funds do you need to see yourself and any dependants through the job-hunting period and/or get certified to practise in your chosen field?

- ▶ The cost of living of your desired or destination city.

- ▶ Tax rates – Australia has high income tax rates. Sales tax (GST) is currently 10%, with threats that it may increase. The Australian Tax Office is the best place to visit to learn more about rates: www.ato.gov.au.

- Holiday leave – the standard local allowance by law is 20 days per year. Note that, according to the National Employment Standards, holiday is accrued over time depending on hours worked and cannot be taken unless you are in 'credit' with your leave time or choose to take unpaid leave.

- Private school fees – these can range from AU$4,000–$25,000 per child, per year. Depending on the state and your visa status, you need to pay to access the public schooling system, so you will need to consider if you are required to pay for your child(ren)'s education.

- Childcare – in great shortage in most urban areas in Australia and costly.

- Spousal support – consider loss of second income for the duration of your assignment or until your spouse is able to secure employment.

- Accommodation – short and long-term allowance. Decent short-term accommodation in urban Australia can start from $100 upwards nightly. Rents are costly also and, when advertised, are expressed as a cost per week. It is the norm for properties to be offered unfurnished.

- Flights – annual flights home for the family, in addition to the relocation flights.

- Relocation – shipping your effects, car, pets, etc. can be time-consuming and costly.

- Cultural coaching – depending on your comfort levels with your new environment, cultural assimilation will assist with the transition for the whole family. Workplace culture, especially, can be surprisingly different to that in the UK.

- Medical Insurance – can cost upwards of $100 per month

per family member. This serves to further subsidise medical costs along with the government's Medicare scheme.

- ► Car – is it included with your employment package or to be imported from the UK (restrictions apply)? Car ownership in Australia is costly, with petrol prices on the rise.

- ► Pension (called 'superannuation' in Australia) – this can be moved back to the UK with you, less tax and within certain time limits of your departure or visa expiry.

- ► General cost of living – like for like, almost everything is more expensive in Australia: food, clothing, car ownership, appliances, furniture...

COST OF LIVING

Accommodation is, for most, the majority of their outgoings. A visit to www.domain.com.au or www.realestate.com.au and a quick search for rents in your preferred areas will help provide a guide to what you can expect to pay. www.cityhobo.com is another great resource – a whole website with detailed information on the five main capital cities and a breakdown of the personality of each city's suburbs and areas. Remember that rents are advertised weekly, not monthly.

Working out the cost of living is difficult given everyone's circumstances are different, and much will depend on where you choose to live, how much you earn, your outgoings, any children you have, and whether you choose to use public transport or buy a car, not to mention varying tastes and expectations in terms of your consumption. A large and badly insulated house with a pool is going to cost considerably more to run than a brand new apartment, for example; although the apartment may initially be more expensive to rent or purchase depending on its location.

The Numbeo website can be useful in summarising indicative numbers around the cost of living: www.numbeo.com.

EXPECTED SALARY IN AUSTRALIA

The www.salaryexpectation.com website is a good place to start to help compare your current salary with what you might expect to earn in Australia.

Recruiters conduct annual salary surveys – note that some will be restricted to industries and roles that they cater for – giving a good indication of what your skills could be worth in Australia:

www.michaelpage.com.au/salarycentre
www.roberthalf.com.au/salary-guides
www.hays.com.au/salary-guide

MOVING COSTS – FURTHER CONSIDERATIONS

Regardless of your earnings once established in Australia, you need to consider the cost of the move and the initial outlay you can expect in the first few weeks of your stay. There are set-up costs with any move, and you may need to pay for accommodation for a number of weeks before you see your first salary payment. Note that you will unlikely be able to obtain a credit card in Australia, so you will need to allow for this in your bank account unless you are using UK funds via a credit card.

Leaving the UK will involve costs that you may not think about when you consider this move. Here is a checklist of some of the likely outgoings you can expect before you arrive in Australia:

	Your estimate
Migration agent fees	
Visa fees	
Shipment and marine insurance	
Flights and travel insurance	
Cost of exploration trips to Australia	
Leaving party	
Pet moving costs, plus customs fees	
Car shipment costs to Australia	
Property fees: selling home or mortgage change	
Final utility bills	
Clear outstanding debt	
Temporary car and accommodation	
TOTAL REQUIRED	

Consider the following as a guide when calculating the set-up costs for your first few months. This is not a definitive list, but it should serve as an indication of outlay. Also note that some items may not be required for your circumstances:

	Your estimate
Temporary accommodation	
Three months of rent: two months to cover the bond deposit and one month's rent in advance. Remember, rental prices are generally advertised	
Council tax (if your house is purchased)	
Foxtel (Satellite, or Pay TV)	
Emergency fund and/or travel insurance	
Insurance – motor	
Insurance – home	
Temporary transport or hire car	
Purchasing a car	
Petrol	
Mobile phone	
Entertainment, going out, having fun	
Appliances, home furnishings (remember, most rentals are unfurnished)	
Gym or sports memberships	
Driving licence (if you are a Permanent Resident (PR))	
Temporary furniture package depending on when your shipment arrives	
TOTAL REQUIRED	

Personal hopes and dreams

Most Brits would give their proverbial right arm to live in Australia, with the promise of a dream lifestyle and lots of sunshine. There is a tantalising opportunity to explore a different culture (not only Australia but the immediate Asia Pacific region), travel a different side of the world, and be exposed to different people, lifestyle, and career opportunities. No doubt about it, the experience would be life-changing. It is, however, not for everyone – and may not be the right choice at a given time.

In addition to all of the above considerations, personal goals such as marriage, having (more) children, pets, or exploring hobbies/lifestyle choices should cross your radar for serious consideration. Consider your bucket list – how would a move to Australia fit into your life? How would it impact on or impede any of your future plans?

Professional hopes and dreams

In general terms, a move abroad mostly serves to enhance your career, and overseas experience can be highly sought after. This can also apply to the spouse who follows you. International exposure is seldom a bad thing.

Things to consider here are the opportunities in your chosen field and the experience and goals you would achieve during your stay in Australia, should you return to the UK. Having a role in Australia firmly imprinted on your CV will likely make a unique talking point for future career endeavours.

On the flip-side, are there likely to be missed opportunities in your industry or chosen field? If so, what are the opportunity costs, if any? You may have unique experience or your industry may be in a unique set of circumstances whereby the timing just isn't right. If your move is a corporate relocation, ensure that there is a repatriation plan in place – or, if you would like to stay in Australia, what allowances will be made? All of this should be considered.

Wants, needs, must-haves, and compromises

After a thorough process of due diligence and deciding whether this move is right for you, the next step is to look forward and consider what your new life might be like. It is also important to consider whether you want to manage this project on your own, or whether you feel some help would be useful. From visa compliance to lifestyle advice, help is available and can make a world of difference to the experience of moving and the start you have.

Financial and lifestyle considerations will be key to working out what you want your life to look like, and being confident about the budget you have for this move is crucial to this step.

Ask yourself:

- ▶ What help will you need along the way? What are you able to do yourself? Should you enlist the help of a relocation professional to help with the process?

- ▶ Where do you want to live? If you're moving with work, this may not be a choice – you may also be restricted by visa and/or budget requirements.

- Which aspects of your current life would you like to transport to Australia?
- What are you hoping to get out of your time in Australia?
- Do you want a house or apartment?
- What commute time is acceptable?
- Do you want a car, or will you use public transport?
- Do you need/want outdoor space at home?
- Which activities are important to you? Gym, hobbies, etc.
- How many bedrooms do you need?
- What schooling do you want for your children?
- Is your spouse planning to work, or to be home-based?
- Do you have pets, or want a pet? If so, you may wish to be near parks and need a garden or outdoor space.

MUST YOU VISIT AUSTRALIA BEFORE YOU LAND?

If you're relocating with work, you may well not have had the chance to visit Australia. You had possibly not even considered visiting, let alone moving there for a period of your life. I would suggest that, if budget and time allows, it's always a good idea to pay a visit to at least find your bearings and get a taste of what to expect. Scout out some areas, have a nose around the shops, visit open house inspections. Open house inspections are a standard way for homes to be viewed by prospective tenants or buyers. Private appointments do exist, but by far the most popular and efficient method is for the home to be 'open' by the estate agent for a set time for all prospects to take a look. On the other hand, if you'll be arriving for the first time, it won't do any harm to have a couple of weeks before you start work to acclimatise and enjoy your new surroundings.

Many people can't believe that we'd never been to Australia before deciding to emigrate here. I have a simple philosophy when making life decisions. I mostly determine whether I'm likely to regret not doing something when an opportunity presents itself. I knew that even if I had visited Australia, this would always be different than actually committing to the culture and lifestyle. I knew that I would look back and regret it if I was still in the UK years on from that juncture, wondering 'What If?'

Now, this is not to say that this approach is right for everyone, and the more people I talk to, the more I have learnt that the approach we took was the exception rather than the norm! I recall the words 'brave', 'crazy', and 'mad' being used many a time when telling people of how we made this life-changing decision. Many people decide to sample the lifestyle after visiting friends or coming on holiday and falling in love with Australia.

Chapter re-cap - **ready, set...**

+ Look at the timing of this move in the context of your life plans, and the length of time the process will take. Does this move fit in with your personal and professional goals?

+ A key consideration is: how will you gain the legal right to live and work in Australia?

+ Financial planning and security is critical. A move Down Under can be costly, and a successful move will involve adequate funds, thorough research, and careful planning.

+ Staying connected with those you leave behind needn't hold you back from this decision. However, spare a thought about the financial and emotional impact of the distance. Then have fun thinking about how it can work, with the help of technology and travel.

+ Be prepared for how your immediate family will cope with the transition, and think about the loved ones you are leaving behind. Weigh up how

>>

you feel about what you'll be missing out on with how the new experience and adventure will factor into your life.

+ Do you need to pay a visit to Australia before deciding if this move is right for you?

+ How are you feeling? After reading this chapter, you should have a clear idea of whether this move is viable for you, and what you need to consider. Emotionally, you might be excited but apprehensive, daunted but optimistic.

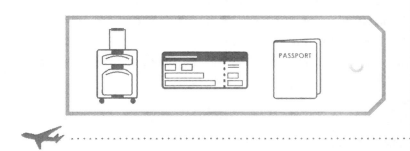

STEP 2
EMBARK

Any substantial journey involves planning and paperwork. An international relocation is infinitely more complex and involves time and consideration of your circumstances and the intricacies involved. I would suggest treating the move like any large project. You will ultimately need a list of actions, each allocated to a responsible party, with an expected timeline for each task.

This chapter focuses on the planning of your move, through to your departure. This can be as little as a few weeks before you move to Australia, if you're relocating with work, to as long as two years if you are planning on achieving permanent residency. You will have to deal with logistical, financial, and administrative matters. I have outlined a list of the items most families and/or individuals will need to consider in preparation for their move, in suggested timeframes of when you might tackle each task.

You've decided you're moving. Expect a waterfall of emotions once the initial excitement passes. Everyone says that moving is one of the most stressful experiences we go through in life. Transferring your life to the other side of the world – that certainly gives you more to consider!

Prepare to feel some or all of the following emotions: excitement, nervousness, anxiety, apprehension, frustration, impatience, sadness, stress, eagerness, fear... the list goes on. You'll be wondering if you've made the right decision, how it will impact your life, and whether you'll be ready – logistically and emotionally. There will be excitement about experiencing the images we all see of Australia – the endless beaches, beautiful produce, and perpetual sunshine. You'll have a sense of personal achievement and anticipate the personal journey and emotional growth that you will experience over the coming period in your life. In fact, you'll experience a rollercoaster of highs and lows.

There are many ways to handle both the positive and negative emotions. My advice is not to ignore what you are feeling – it is completely natural. Remember that you're not alone – every expat has experienced this at some stage.

Here are some tips to help you manage the emotions and ensure your energy is used productively:

- ▶ Understand that this is normal.

- ▶ Think positively – this is an amazing opportunity and will be life-changing.

- ▶ Plan and research – the success of your relocation will be dependent on many variables – financials, the people you meet, how well you manage to adapt, and so on. It is absolutely key to plan effectively and to have a good idea what to expect. Managing to predict and plan as much as possible will help give you confidence and at least an element of certainty during a very uncertain time.

► Have a departure plan and create a list. List everything that you need to do before you leave and attach a deadline to each item. Having a clear plan of tasks and goals will help keep you focused – and knowing that everything is in hand ensures there are fewer variables to stress you out.

► Develop your arrival plan – put together your list of things to do when you land to make sure you're ready to get on with living and settling in.

► Set a date for your move and research flights.

Don't forget to reach out – to join forums online, and to seek advice from anyone you might know who has lived in Australia or is currently doing so. Much of any anxiety or stress you may have is fear of the unknown. A perspective from someone whose opinion you trust really can make a great deal of difference.

As soon as possible

PETS

The process of moving your pet is actually straightforward, but it is crucial to start your research as soon as possible. Australia is fiercely protective of its borders and the flora and fauna within them. It therefore takes a lot of form filling and time to navigate this, not to mention the obligatory quarantine period. You may choose to use an agent or company to help manage this. These experts are usually well worth the investment to ensure a smooth transition for your pet. Do note that regardless of whether you choose to outsource the task or do it yourself, the process of importing and quarantine will be costly. It's important to start to understand the process involved. You can visit the Australian Government's Department of Agriculture website at www.daff.gov.au and search for pets. This will also provide you with a calculator outlining all of the steps and timings associated with moving your pet to Australia.

Visit the Traveler's Pet Corner at www.iata.org/whatwedo/cargo/live-animals/pets/Pages/index.aspx for a guide on what you can expect for your pet in relation to the long journey.

Up to 24 months prior to departure

VISA, PASSPORT, AND INDUSTRY REGISTRATIONS

The number one priority is to ensure your visa application is underway and that you are clear on the requirements, registrations, or licences required to work in your chosen profession. Depending on whether you are moving with your employer or under your own steam, this can take anywhere from a few weeks to two years, depending on your circumstances and the backlog.

Whilst waiting for your visa to be approved, make sure that your passport is valid for at least one year. If you have a few months of validity left, it's usually possible to add the extra months to your new passport rather than lose them. If your passport expires before your visa, you will need to carry your new passport along with the old one until you are able to have the visa transferred to your new passport. Applying for a UK passport renewal in Australia is common practice and a straightforward, if time-consuming, process.

Make sure that you know the visa's validation date – this is essentially a deadline by which you need to enter Australia to validate your visa. It cannot be moved and is not flexible. Once it is validated (i.e. you have a stamp saying you met the required entry date), you can come and go as you please for the duration of the visa.

Six months prior to departure – deal with your possessions

PROPERTY AND CAR

If you rent a property in the UK, you will simply need to serve the notice period and/or penalty as appropriate. Consider the timing of this carefully in order that you have a home until you need to depart.

Owning a property in the UK, assuming you live in it, leaves you with two options. Sell, or lease it to a tenant. There is a third – leave it empty, but most of us don't have that preference or luxury.

Selling your property may take time and may be complicated, depending on the timing of your move. Estate agents in your area should be able to advise on the level of enquiry for your type of property, which can guide your course of action and decision making.

Should you wish to lease your property, it is crucial to check the terms of your mortgage to ensure that you are not in breach in any way. A word of warning - mortgage agreements will differ in terms of whether you must occupy or can let your property, so check that you comply and settle this with your lender before leaving the UK. I have heard firsthand stories of property owners who have landed in Australia only to be notified by their lender that they are in serious breach of their mortgage agreement as they had not advised them of the home's rental status. This is something best dealt with proactively rather than on the other side of the world.

Letting your property will give you a chance to keep furniture or items that you may not choose to bring with you. The 'Packing' section in this chapter will help you decide which possessions to bring and help with this quandary.

If you own a car and are not considering taking it to Australia, you will need to sell or have a plan of what to do with it. Perhaps a friend or relative is interested in acquiring it; otherwise, you will need to advertise it for sale in the classifieds, or get valuations for a car dealer to purchase it from you. If you lease a car, you will need to advise the leasing company and make necessary arrangements to end the agreement and settle any penalties, if applicable.

Whether you choose to ship your car will depend on its value and your circumstances. There are stipulations as to ownership for a period before you ship it, so it is best to speak with your shipper or another company with plenty of experience in this regard. Be prepared for an abundance of paperwork, duties, taxes, import fees, and possible cleaning costs. Note that you should investigate the insurance of the car for when you arrive. Some insurance companies may classify your car differently or have restrictions on what they will cover due to it being purchased and maintained overseas.

Either way, this will require time and some planning, so it is best to start this sooner rather than later. You can then have enough time to wrap up matters of insurance, clearing finance debt, and passing on the registration and licencing as appropriate.

PACKING – DECIDING WHAT TO BRING

Any move is an ideal opportunity to rationalise your possessions. The cathartic process of 'cull and de-clutter' ensures that you minimise any storage logistics back in the UK and reduce the volume of the shipment to Australia.

This process is important. It may be tempting to start afresh and buy everything new. On the flipside, you may feel it best to bring everything to minimise any outlay when you arrive. I suggest that somewhere in between is the right amount!

Based on my experience and the customs regulations, here is an overview of the key items we all need for the smooth running of a home and lifestyle, along with information you will find useful when going through your inventory.

BEDS AND LINEN

No special commentary here – if you love your bed and it's worth the price to ship it, there will be one less item needed to furnish your new home.

Beds are sized and named slightly differently in the UK. In general, a Queen size in Australia is equivalent to the UK King, and Australia's King size bed is called a Super King in the UK.

Cushion, or pillow top, beds are popular here, and the bed linen ('Manchester' as it's called here) follows suit, so you are able to buy deeper sided bed sheets.

CLOTHES

The climate here will require a slight re-think of your wardrobe. You'll inevitably need more in the way of summer or warm weather clothes and less bulky items for winter. That is not to say that gloves, scarves, and coats won't be needed – they will be for at least two to three months of the year. Depending on your profession, office attire here is unlikely to differ significantly to the UK.

Due to the heat, especially in the height of summer, you will end up wearing more casual clothing and swimwear, so it's best to bring this all along with you or pack it into your shipment to meet you here.

ELECTRICAL ITEMS AND APPLIANCES

Large appliances may be worth bringing, depending on their age and whether they will survive the move. Washing machines and dryers are generally not included with properties for sale or rent.

Fridges have coolant in them, which is subject to import restrictions. It's best to check with your shipping company to determine the latest regulations. This will help you decide whether it's worth moving yours or purchasing a new one on arrival.

Other smaller items, such as hairdryers, lamps, and TVs, should travel well and may be worth bringing to save the financial outlay of replacing them on arrival. Note that you may wish to bring a number of multi-plugs and converter plugs to get through your first few weeks or months. You can then decide which items should be converted to Australian plugs.

Note that Australian TV broadcasts require a digital receiver. If your TV doesn't have one, you will need to purchase one on arrival for a small cost – or consider replacing your TV with a new one when you arrive (which should have it built in). Televisions and most electronics are not much more expensive compared to the UK.

Essential once you arrive will be an unlocked mobile phone. I would suggest bringing one if possible. Alternatively, you can buy one on arrival to ensure you stay connected. Setting up mobile phone access is quick and straightforward, so get yourself a local SIM card as soon as is practicable. You can use your UK line and access, but bear in mind that this will be expensive due to international roaming charges. It's prudent to forewarn loved ones and important contacts that you are best reached via email during your travel period, and advise them of your new number on arrival. If at all feasible, a smartphone with internet access is highly recommended to help with all of the communications and searches you will need to make whilst out and about and establishing yourself in the first weeks and beyond.

FURNITURE

This forms a large chunk of the budget in making a house feel like a home. Furniture can be expensive in Australia, so, if you have valuable furniture, I would advise storing it or bringing it with you. The likes of IKEA exist here at similarly reasonable prices, so any of your cheaper furniture will probably not be worth shipping if it can be replaced here.

Outdoor furniture, if precious to you, will be worth bringing to help settle into the more outdoorsy lifestyle out here.

Beware that any wooden items or furniture will have to be declared and are subject to fumigation or other cleaning fees if deemed necessary. This will be at your cost.

PLANTS AND OTHER PERISHABLES

These are, without doubt, best left in the UK. You will need permits to bring plants into the country, so, unless of sentimental or high monetary value, donate them to friends and family. Similarly, perishables will have to be declared and may be confiscated.

SPORTS EQUIPMENT

If you're a skier, you may wish to bring your gear with you – it surprises many that there is a ski season here, albeit at lower altitude and with less reliable snow than in the Alps, for example. Many choose to travel to NZ, Japan, the US, or even back to Europe to get their fix if not satisfied with the Aussie offering.

Cyclists and golfers should bring their equipment over, although be prepared to declare this and face possible fees to disinfect or fumigate if there is a perceived risk of disease – i.e. via mud or grass.

Any water-sport equipment – surf board, kayak – would be at home in Australia. Ensure you bring it, as there will be ample opportunity for its use.

Everything that you choose not to bring will need to be dealt with. There are various avenues to shed unwanted items – eBay, garage sales, charitable giving, friends and family, etc. This process will take discipline and time, so it's key to start as soon as possible.

ARRANGING YOUR SHIPMENT

Along with flights, shipping your effects will likely account for a large portion of your moving budget.

Once you've decided on what to take, the first port of call will be to choose companies that will provide a quote based on your needs. It's always advisable to check quality and industry accreditations of the company you intend to use. Start with these industry bodies:

www.bar.co.uk or www.baroverseas.co.uk
www.fidi.org

Your life's belongings will be taken care of by the company you choose, so peace of mind is key.

The process of getting a quote can take time, so I would suggest getting this a.s.a.p. for budgeting purposes. You can then decide the date to book in the move. Note that, if you wish to insure your shipment (highly recommended), the shipping company will likely insist that they do all of the packing themselves.

I would suggest getting three quotes. Ensure that you do like-for-like comparisons, as each company's costs will be presented in different ways.

Things to think about and ask your shipping company:

- ▶ How long will the shipment take?

- ▶ Are you able to track the shipment?

- ▶ What is their pricing structure? Is it fixed pricing, or pro rata according to volume?

- ▶ How much is the insurance? What will it cover?

- ▶ Do they organise packing? If so, how long will it take? Are all of the packing materials included?

- ▶ If you require storage at any stage, what is the fee?

- ▶ Does the fee include quarantine and customs clearance? I would strongly advise that you enlist their help with this – the red tape involved is best handled by the professionals.

- ▶ What industry accreditations do they have?

The cost will predominantly depend on the volume of possessions and the insurance coverage. For an additional fee, most will organise unpacking when the shipment arrives. Depending on how 'stuck in' you intend to be, this might be a good idea to minimise disruption.

Ensure you keep a comprehensive inventory (required to insure your items anyway) – it's surprising how many items you'll unpack at the other end and forgot you had!

Depending on your plans between departing the UK and landing in Australia, do ensure you have all of your vital paperwork with you and enough clothing to keep you going when you arrive. It is advisable that you compile at least two working files – one for the UK-related departure; the other ready for your arrival in Australia.

Four months prior to departure – the bookings for your arrival

Getting organised will involve committing to bookings. Depending on your timeline, you may wish to line up school and property viewings ready for your arrival.

CAR RENTAL

Hiring a car on landing in Australia is not the cost effective option it may seem. Car rental companies conveniently placed in the airport charge a premium. Most likely, you will be staying centrally on arrival, and my suggestion would be to get a taxi to your accommodation. Spend a day or two acclimatising and getting over the jet lag, then you can think about renting a car from a central location. All of the global car hire companies are represented in Australia, with a few local options which may be more cost effective.

FLIGHTS

Booking your flight provides you with a milestone and deadline. Both daunting and exciting!

These days, one-way flights are often as cost effective as half of the return price, so, if you are unsure about when you'd like to return to the UK or prefer to minimise your costs, you can always book a one-way ticket. One-way fares can start from as low as £500, and the sky is the limit if you want to turn left rather than right when you get off the plane!

You can fly via the USA to take advantage of the double luggage allowance, but this is a long journey option. The fastest way to get to Australia is via the Middle East or Asia with a range of airlines including Emirates, Cathay Pacific, Singapore Airlines, and the Australian national airline, Qantas. Flights between the UK and Australia are frequent and often book out far in advance, especially during school holidays in either country.

Either way, you can choose to stop over to break up the journey. The shortest journey time is typically 24 hours, which includes a two-hour stopover for refuelling and/or transiting. Needless to say, this is a gruelling trip, and I personally prefer to break with at least one stopover. Whilst I was chomping at the bit to start my new life in Australia, I had a hankering for some travel and so flew via the USA for a fortnight before landing in Sydney. This really is down to personal choice and when you prefer to get started in your new life.

Airlines all have their own flight booking options online, or you can choose to shop around at a plethora of travel agents that may offer interesting discounts given their buying power. Agencies such as Flight Centre and STA Travel exist in Australia as well as the UK and sometimes guarantee lowest fares.

PROPERTY AND SCHOOL VIEWINGS

The vast majority of properties available for rent or sale will be advertised on either of these property listing websites: www.domain.com.au or www.realestate.com.au. Viewings (also called inspections) are very short and tend to be towards the end of the week.

School viewings and appointments are advisable. Private school registrars are usually accommodating and understand that expats have tight timeframes in which to make decisions and enrol in a school. Appointments should be relatively straightforward to organise.

Government funded schools, on the other hand, are not obliged to accept your child unless you reside in their catchment area. Note that highly subscribed schools, in a worst-case scenario, may insist on a fixed address with your rental contract as evidence before they will entertain you. It is also common to have fixed open days for prospective parents, so it pays to investigate this in advance and plan accordingly.

SHORT-TERM ACCOMMODATION

Putting a roof over your head for your initial arrival can be expensive but is often a necessary first stop whilst you hunt for a longer-term option. Hotels, short-term holiday rentals, and serviced apartments are options with varying levels of investment. Depending on how brave you are feeling and when in the year you are arriving, I would advise a minimum of one week. You can check whether a longer booking is permissible with your provider on the proviso that you cut it short should you be lucky enough to find a permanent option quickly.

Accommodation danger zones tend to be school holidays and the long summer holiday from mid-December until the end of January.

www.wotif.com is a useful hotel-booking tool which aggregates the best deals. Some serviced apartments and other options like hostels will offer their accommodation here too.

www.stayz.com.au and the newer www.airbnb.com connect guests with property owners who wish to let on a short-term basis, usually a minimum of two to three nights.

Serviced apartment chains such as Quest, Meriton, Adina, and Oaks are comfortable options that are usually well positioned. Depending on the city, there will be a range of local options which may suit your needs. Here are some websites to help you get started:

www.questapartments.com.au
www.meritonapartments.com.au
www.adinahotels.com.au
www.oakshotelsresorts.com.au

TRAVEL INSURANCE

This is always advisable, and a large relocation is no exception. Not only do I advise that your shipment is fully insured, your travels to Australia should also be covered in the event of any luggage loss, flight cancellations, or other unexpected occurrences.

Two months prior to departure – administration and mental preparation

Ensuring that you wrap things up in the UK is important for closure and to minimise unnecessary and distracting communications in your new home. You will need to cancel standing orders and direct debits and to settle debts and final bills. You also need to advise relevant authorities and companies of your new address, or that you no longer wish to receive their mailings. This will be a challenge given you may not know where you will be living. My suggestion here would be to seek out a generous family member or friend who is willing to receive your mail on your behalf.

This list is a good starting point for most. It's a good idea, once you know you are moving, to start building a list of all of the post you receive to help with this process, and to minimise the risk of missing anything.

- ▶ Bank and other investments
- ▶ Car finance
- ▶ Car insurance
- ▶ Car licencing and registration
- ▶ Council tax
- ▶ Credit cards
- ▶ Dentist
- ▶ Doctor
- ▶ DVLA
- ▶ Gas, electricity, and water – final meter readings
- ▶ HM Revenue & Customs
- ▶ Home insurance
- ▶ Home phone and broadband
- ▶ Life insurance
- ▶ Magazine subscriptions
- ▶ Medical insurance
- ▶ Mobile phone
- ▶ Mortgage
- ▶ Newspaper subscriptions
- ▶ Optician
- ▶ Pension company
- ▶ Store and other loyalty cards
- ▶ TV licence
- ▶ Your current employer(s)

ESSENTIAL PAPERWORK

Your first weeks in Australia will involve lots of registrations and associated form filling. Much of it will be related to proving your identity; other documentation will be required as reference points. Ensure that you have all of the information necessary to access it – passwords and so on – in these days of online accessibility. It's useful to keep these in a central file for easy access over this busy period. I strongly advise that you hand carry this file with you on the flight to have it available when needed to minimise risk of it going astray. This is the time to create a central storage point for the paperwork you have been gathering.

Another good idea is to have electronic copies or access to these files. A great resource is an online or cloud storage space such as Dropbox or Skydrive. These can be accessed anywhere and can offer valuable peace of mind in the knowledge that a simple internet connection can provide most of what you need.

The following list is a general starting point of what to keep in your central file. You will have other documents specific to your circumstances.

- ▶ Passports
- ▶ Flight tickets
- ▶ All bookings information for Australia arrival
- ▶ Birth certificates
- ▶ Marriage certificate
- ▶ Medical records and prescriptions, latest eye-test results
- ▶ Driving licence
- ▶ Academic records – university degrees, children's test results, professional qualifications, and certificates

- Bank details – UK and Australia
- Pension information
- Insurance documents
- Shipment documents, inventory, and insurance documents
- P45 – a record of tax you've paid given to you at end of your employment
- P85 – HM Revenue & Customs form used to claim tax relief when you depart the UK
- CV
- Landlord/tenancy references
- Proof of final UK bill payments and debt settlements
- Copy of utility bills to attest to your credit history

It is important also to have contact information to hand the many people you will be speaking to during this process:

- Shipping company, including pet or car shipment agencies
- UK landlord
- UK employer
- UK bank
- Currency broker
- Australia bank
- Travel agent or airline
- Accommodation you have booked
- Car rental you have organised
- UK doctor – obtain any prescription medications for your first few weeks in Australia
- Schools
- Prospective employers, recruitment agents
- Contacts in Australia that you have been introduced to

FINANCIALS

You will have decided that you can afford to make this move, will understand your budget, and have a target of when you need to be earning a salary and can settle into your new routine. By now, the financial matters should be mostly administrative. Ensuring you are compliant from a tax perspective and knowing how to efficiently move and manage your money will be top of mind.

Setting up an Australian bank account may be something you'd prefer to do before arriving. The likes of HSBC are international and you should be able to set this up with ease from the UK. Westpac and Commonwealth Bank are two examples of Australian banks that offer the setup of your bank account before you arrive in Australia. Note that until you provide them with the 100 points of identification (more on this in Step 4), you can only make deposits into your account. Once you have proven your identity, you will have a fully operational Aussie bank account.

For substantial transfers into Australian currency, you may prefer to shop around for a currency broker. These can be much cheaper than a standard bank transfer of one currency to another, so it is worth exploring for larger amounts of money. HIFX at www.hifx.com.au is a popular choice, and there are many others you can choose from. Money laundering and other financial crime means that you need to undergo a verification process to be fully up and running. Once you are set up, money can be transferred over the phone and the transaction can be completed in a matter of days.

You should consider the amount of money you will need to manage your first few weeks. Finding a rental property alone will require one month's rent as a bond deposit plus one month's rent in advance, which can amount to a lot of money. It may be necessary for you to offer a few months' rent in advance, depending on your circumstances and how easily you are able to prove your income source to honour your rental agreement. Other setup incidentals should also be accounted for in this initial fund to ensure you can comfortably handle your setup outgoings in the early days.

In addition to getting set up for Aussie life, it's a good idea to close off debt or to line up arrangements to manage this in your absence. It is common to still have access to your UK credit card, and managing accounts online is the standard these days. Just ensure that you are receiving bills and reminders to meet your deadlines, as, in my experience, 'out of sight, out of mind' can apply when you're busy settling in to your new home.

It's unfortunate that, despite any best efforts, your credit rating will unlikely follow you from the UK. The usual prompt payment of bills, having a regular salary, and having a credit in your bank account all contribute to this over time. It is advisable to put joint names or a non-working spouse's name on utility bills to help build this rating. You will be reminded about this in Step 3.

Your UK private pension should be able to tick along and be managed in your absence. Moving it to Australia is fairly straightforward if you wish to do this – though do seek out a financial adviser who has expertise in this area. Otherwise, it's important to ensure that you have a means to manage it and can communicate with your fund in your absence.

It is possible to keep contributing to the state pension system by making National Insurance contributions whilst abroad. Contact HM Revenue & Customs for more information relating to your circumstances, as there are specific criteria and instructions. This is especially important if you are likely to return to the UK.

As with all matters financial and otherwise outlined here, it's advisable to seek professional advice relating to your personal circumstances.

NOTICE PERIOD

Ensure that your exit has been planned with your employer, with a clear date of when you can expect your final salary payment and P45. You may be eligible to receive tax back (after completing a P85 form), depending on the time of year you will stop working. This could be a welcome boost to your relocation budget.

SAYING GOODBYE

Moving abroad is a huge achievement and should be celebrated. It's a milestone that you and your loved ones should be proud of, but saying goodbye is never easy. A few months or an uncertain period will pass before you are reunited with those you care about. Ensure that you capture the moments and that your friends and family have an opportunity to send you off.

Set a date for a big party, or arrange smaller gatherings within your final week or fortnight. If you're lucky, a friend or family member may even help to arrange this for you. This process will also give you something to look forward to as a reward for all of your hard work and stress in anticipation of the move.

TAX MATTERS AND REFUNDS

All tax matters need to be settled and dealt with in the UK before you leave. The logistics of handling these issues will cause undue extra stress if you move to Australia without wrapping everything up.

Tax is always best acknowledged. If you intend to work full-time abroad for one or more tax years (6 April–5 April) or, indeed, you intend to move away permanently, you must advise HM Revenue & Customs. Otherwise, you run the risk of being liable for UK tax as well as tax in Australia.

If you are leaving part way through the tax year, you may also be eligible for a tax refund. Note that this is all dependent on what your employer has withheld from your salary – well worth investigating.

When you stop working, your employer will issue a P45, which is a declaration of your earnings and the tax paid by your employer against it. Should you be eligible for a tax refund, you will need to complete the form P85 as soon as possible.

For more information or queries about this in relation to your circumstances, contact HM Revenue & Customs: www.hmrc.gov.uk.

WISH LIST – YOUR PERSONAL GOALS

In addition to the essential accommodation and flight bookings, it's good for your morale to think about the fun and 'exploratory' aspects of your new surroundings. Everyone needs a break from the grind and stress of settling into a new place, so it's a great idea to start thinking about what you'd like to get out of the first weeks and months of your new life – whether it be beginning to put your routine in place or making some new discoveries.

I had grand ideas when I arrived that the move would be a great opportunity to change my career, spend more time outdoors, learn how to sail, live by the water, and travel every few weekends to somewhere new. What I soon learnt was that the myriad of things I wanted to accomplish was at best ambitious, and at worst putting pressure on me to re-invent my life completely, with no sense of routine and normality. Too many variables made my first few months miserable once the move happened and I had found a job. I simply wanted to 'make the most' of everything. This was exhausting and inevitably my expectations of what I 'should' be doing were not met. Moving is new and exciting, but it is imperative to keep a sense of routine and normality to keep you grounded and to pace yourself into your new life.

This will look different to everyone, so it's worth first considering the aspects of your life that are non-negotiable and crucial for you being happy and settled on a day-to-day basis. Things like your hobbies and interests, sports, study, and socialising will be top of mind here. What does your ideal week look like outside of work? It may be a visit to the gym or a having a run, playing a team sport, playing in a band, exploring new bars, cooking, etc. Whatever it is, invest time in thinking about how you might build a routine that will keep your mind and body stimulated during these initial stages of moving.

Australia is a great country in which to explore a different lifestyle, so it can be motivating to begin thinking about a wish list of activities or 'must-sees' during your stay. Have you always wanted to dive in the Great Barrier Reef? Or to learn how to surf, play a new sport, take up a new hobby, or visit each corner of this vast country? Create a bucket list, and ensure that you keep on top of all the things you want to get out of your life here. Ensure that your first few months are peppered with a few of these activities or goals. This will enhance your life here and allow other, unexpected opportunities to be explored without the pressure of completely re-defining your life.

Two weeks prior to departure – prepare to arrive

BUY CURRENCY

This is an important consideration; make sure that you're not caught out on arrival. It's worth getting enough Australian Dollars for at least the first week or so. You may prefer not to carry much cash, but bear in mind that your bank account here will require an address for complete setup (details in Step 4), so perhaps consider using a UK credit card in addition to cash in the interim.

Another convenient option is to buy a 'Money Card' or currency card. This is basically a card that you credit with up to five or ten currencies, for use pretty much anywhere that accepts a credit card. It also allows you to withdraw cash from a range of cash machines. A few banks sell them, along with the Post Office; an internet search will help to find one that suits your needs.

JOB INTERVIEWS

If you're not moving with your company and a job, it is highly likely that you'll be planning to look for employment. Most recruiters will advise that you wait until arrival, but you may be lucky enough to have one or two with roles that may consider you and book an interview for your arrival. If you have any contacts at all, I would suggest that booking meeting times will be highly beneficial for your morale and may help you to glean useful and local knowledge for subsequent interviews and negotiations.

Chapter re-cap – **up, up, and away...**

+ This phase of the move can be overwhelming. There's much to do at a time when you will experience a raft of both positive and negative emotions. All of this is completely normal. It's important at this stage to focus on the task at hand; devise a clear timeline and outline of your priorities.

+ Time to get organised. If this is not your strength and/or you simply don't have the time to deal with this, enlist the help of a relocation specialist to manage some, or all, of the process for you.

+ Get the house and your possessions in check – what will you be getting rid of, leaving behind, taking with you? Make sure you get quotes from reputable companies to ship your items.

+ Does your home need to be sold or must you provide notice for your rental property?

+ Set a date for your move and organise all of the flights, accommodation, and other planning around it.

>>

+ Research and think of some fun things you'd like to do when you arrive to break up the routine of the move, and get your finances and paperwork in order.

+ How are you feeling? You might be suffering from anticipatory stress, nervousness, and possible sadness at what lies ahead. Don't forget to seek help and support, if needed, and know that these feelings are normal.

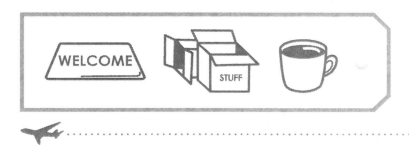

STEP 3

TAKE UP RESIDENCE

You've arrived! The weeks and months of planning have passed, and you're living and breathing the checklist. The focus of getting things done will be a welcome distraction. There is a sense of excitement at wanting to explore your new surroundings, although you're missing home and are feeling a little anxious and scared. At the same time you'll feel disorientated and at times frustrated with having to navigate a new system to get settled in and compliant with all the paperwork and practicalities.

This step is all about finding a place to call home and ensuring that you kick off the process of establishing your new life in Australia.

Many of the steps that follow this stage will rely on you having a fixed address and acknowledgement from utility and other companies that you now reside in this country.

Most people will be focused solely on renting a property to start with, though of course this depends on your circumstances. I would suggest if you have not lived in Australia before, it is prudent to rent for the first 6–12 months of your stay. This period will pass very quickly and will give you an opportunity to get an initial taster for your immediate area and beyond. If you have a job before arriving, commute times and other factors will be clearer than if you have no idea where your work will take you.

Be prepared to make quick decisions during this stage of your move, and make sure you cast as wide a net as possible. This applies to your job or home search, or setting up multiple appointments for schools to ensure you gather as much information and knowledge as possible. I find that, whilst exhausting, every conversation you have in the early stages will provide an additional level of knowledge and, ultimately, comfort and confidence. This will help immensely with your sense of belonging.

Staying focused and having a daily routine is key. Build a checklist of tasks and goals for the first few weeks, including a list of all of the paperwork required for each step. Ensure that you prioritise accordingly. For example, finding the nearest hospital and doctor may be most important to you, and I would suggest that this is closely followed by Medicare registration and obtaining a Tax File Number (TFN).

It is worth knowing that most of your property viewings will likely be towards the end of the week. Most estate agents will spend the early part of the week updating listings and finalising applications submitted during the weekend viewings, so you can plan on using Monday–Wednesday for administrative matters, registrations, and other tasks. By this time, property listings will be updated, and agents will be ready to talk about rental inventories and scheduling of inspections.

Make sure you have a 'fun' checklist also – whether it be checking out a new restaurant, sightseeing, or simply exploring supermarkets and shopping areas. These are crucial to ensuring that you feel settled and at home more quickly. Do you enjoy yoga, want to join a gym, or to learn how to surf? Don't put your personal and relaxation needs at the bottom of the list, as these are crucial to your wellbeing. This familiarisation needs to feature as a priority every couple of days or so, ensuring an enjoyable and balanced introduction to your new life.

Arrival

CUSTOMS AND IMMIGRATION

You will most likely receive a friendly welcome to Australia. At the very least, it will be cordial and efficient. Everyone (including PRs and citizens) must complete a form when they arrive into Australia, covering both immigration and the customs declarations. By now, you will realise that Australia is fiercely protective of its borders. Whilst the system is efficient, you may be subject to a long wait at quarantine, depending on the number of flights that have arrived. Ensure that you declare everything you are bringing – you will likely have your luggage x-rayed at the very least. Jars of Marmite, packs of Bisto, and Walkers smoky bacon crisps will not surprise any customs official and will likely give them a giggle.

TRANSPORT AND DRIVING TO YOUR ACCOMMODATION

Every airport will have taxis readily available. Road tolls and airport fees will be in addition to the metered fare. You will likely have plenty of baggage with you, so I suggest this would be the preferred option.

All airports will also have either city shuttle bus or public transport options. Shuttle services are generally privately run companies and can be booked in advance. Depending on the number of passengers, these are generally cost effective for cities like Melbourne and Brisbane, where the airports are a fair distance from the city centre.

Rental car companies are well placed in all of the airports. Note that whilst you will want to rent a car for your stay, I would suggest being car free until you settle in. Observe the driving culture, acclimatise, and be well rested before tackling this new experience. Car rental companies also charge a premium or one-off fee for the privilege of collecting the car from the airport. Rental depots exist in all city centres and will also include more competitive local companies which may offer better rates and/or discounts for longer rentals.

The prospect of the journey to your new abode is deeply exciting – your first foray on Australian soil. You're exhausted from the trip, adrenalin is pumping – your nose will likely be against the window to absorb your new surroundings. The journey will be between 10–50 minutes (10 for Adelaide, 50 for Melbourne, with the other cities somewhere in between) and most likely uneventful. Most routes between the airport and cities are boring – it will only get better from here.

A PLACE TO CALL HOME

Choosing where to live anywhere new is tricky. It's even more daunting in a new country with a life you don't know much about yet.

I would start with basic considerations like where you're likely to work and whether you'll have access to a car for your commute. When we first moved to Sydney, we figured that living centrally would suit us best given we weren't planning on having a car. We were within 15 minutes' walk of the CBD, close to the fish market, cafés, and other amenities – perfect. The fact is, for three to four months of the year, Sydney (and much of Australia) can be unbearably hot. Walking to work, or anywhere beyond five minutes, in a suit or work attire can have severe cosmetic consequences when it's 35°C and the sun is beating down on you! For me, it just wasn't practical, and I ended up having to rethink what would work best for my sanity.

You will have read the overview earlier in this book about the states and their various personalities. Once you have decided which state to live in (assuming you have the choice), you will need to think about your likely day-to-day activities and what you want to get out of your life in Australia.

AREA PROFILES AND AMENITIES

The website localstats.qpzm.com.au provides a good summary of suburb statistics – plenty of useful demographic information which will give you a good idea of what you can expect.

Paired with the demographic information on the site mentioned above, the following site is useful in providing an objective overview of each region and suburb in each of the five main capital cities: www.cityhobo.com.

BUDGET AND LIFESTYLE

Choosing where you live and ensuring you can establish a routine quickly will have a significant impact on your outlook and the time it takes for you to feel at home. The lifestyle you wish to have, and all of the associated activities and amenities to fulfil it, will in part be determined by where you live.

Almost everyone who moves to Australia wants water views and a beach lifestyle. The romance of the serenity of water and prospect of a short walk to the beach are hugely appealing. The reality is that demand outstrips supply. Pricing, therefore, is at a significant premium and you will get much better bang for your buck elsewhere. This will force you to truly consider what is important to your day-to-day routine and help you to firm up your budget.

What are you hoping to get out of your stay in Australia? Many have ambitious plans to maximise every spare moment doing something new and exciting. You'll learn to surf, water-ski, sail, dive! This is a great objective, but focus on getting your ideal routine in check before racing off and trying new activities, because the novelty factor of too many new and exciting activities can serve to delay the settling-in process. I'm not saying to hold back on any of the 'fun' stuff – of course you'll want to explore and take in your new city and seek out the bits to help it live up to your expectations.

However, it's key that you feel settled and at home. If you enjoy the gym, yoga, swimming, team sports, playing an instrument, knitting – whatever it may be, seek these out as soon as possible after you arrive to derive some sense of normality. Inevitably, you will have days where your energy or morale is low. Routine, and having a go at a hobby or pastime that is 'normal' for you, helps with a sense of belonging.

COMMUTING

Your likely daily commute is an important consideration. If you are planning to work in a professional services capacity, good access to the CBD will probably be crucial. FMCG, pharmaceuticals, and electronic companies tend to be in outlying suburbs where a car becomes a stronger consideration.

There is no 'typical' daily commute time here – it's really down to the lifestyle you aspire to and the budget you can afford. I decided that I would need to commute less than I did when working in London, which was around three hours a day – I figured that half of that would be the maximum I would want to endure.

Driving in rush hour can be arduous in the likes of Sydney and Melbourne, and parking tricky.

FINDING A HOME

Property in Australia is expensive – whether you are planning to rent or buy. The rental markets in all capital cities are tightly held, with demand generally outweighing supply. This applies for the most part to popular and central suburbs in and around the main cities.

The vast majority of properties will be advertised online, with www.domain.com.au and www.realestate.com.au offering a number of functions and tools to help manage the process. Each listing will include whether viewings are private or open inspection, and they are updated as late as a few hours prior to the viewing. The key is to keep your eyes firmly peeled. It can be a full-time job and/or obsession, depending on how in-demand your preferred suburb is. Almost all properties will have a real-estate agent who will act on behalf of the owner/landlord. Saturday newspapers will also have large property pull-out sections advertising viewing times for the day.

The viewings/inspections process is not for the faint-hearted. It requires a tight schedule, a car, and GPS or good map to be competitive. Most inspections in the same suburb will be very close together, and some will overlap so that you'll have to make alternate arrangements for some properties. These can be short for rentals – 15 minutes in some cases. Properties for sale tend to have a longer viewing window of 30 minutes or so.

Private inspections are usually available, but the bulk of properties on both the rental and sales market will have scheduled viewings. It's bizarre and daunting to be faced with your 'competition'. Most agents will arrange private viewings if for some reason you cannot attend the scheduled inspection times. This can provide more of a private insight into the circumstances of the rental or sale that may help your understanding of your 'chances'.

HINTS, TIPS, AND TERMINOLOGIES

- ▶ LUG – lock up garage. Preceded with an 'S' = secure, 'D' = double.

- ▶ Unit – apartment.

- ▶ Robes, BIR – wardrobes, cupboards.

- ▶ STCA – subject to council approval (applies to properties for sale).

- ▶ A/C or reverse cycle A/C – air conditioning – you'll most likely want this with summer temperatures rising to at least 30°C in the summer in most cities, much higher on some days. Central or installed heating is not common in Australia, with the exception of Melbourne where a few properties will have it connected.

- ▶ Property size, if expressed at all, will be in square metres (1 square metre = 10. 76 square feet).

- ▶ Rental rates are expressed as a weekly amount.

- ▶ The bond (security deposit) is one month's or four weeks' rent; it's also required to pay one month's rent in advance. In Australia, the rental bond is held by an independent 3rd party - in most cases the state's fair trading or consumer protection body. This ensures that there is no bias in event of any dispute. At the end of the tenancy, either party can claim against the bond in the case of damage, or not, as the case may be.

- Some highly or oversubscribed public schools will require a copy of a tenancy agreement as proof of residency before they will truly engage with you.

- You may wish to consider offering a few months' rent in advance if you do not have a regular income and want to increase your chances of being approved.

- A condition report will need to be signed and agreed. This will determine what proportion of your bond you will be entitled to, depending on the condition in which you leave the property at the end of your tenancy.

- Appliances such as cooktops, ovens, and dishwashers are generally included with rental properties, and they may be part of the home sale. The fridge, washing machine, and dryer usually aren't, so it's good to bear this in mind. By law, many units will need to provide a clothes dryer if there are no other means to hang or dry clothes.

RENTING A PROPERTY

The rental system in Australia tends to favour owners and landlords. Every rental will require the prospective tenant to complete an application form, with various supporting documents, such as identification, proof of ability to pay, etc. Most rental applications will ask for your offer of rental term and the weekly rent you are prepared to pay – I found this very odd. If you have attended the open-house inspections, this can help you to understand your negotiating power based on the competition or lack thereof. The standard expected rental term is 12 months. This, of course, varies, so it's best to chat with the agent involved to shed light on the landlord's preferences.

You should bring the following supporting documents with you, or have them scanned for emailing. This will ensure you can make an application on the spot, which will more likely be considered:

▶ Copies of passport photo page – all adults in household.

▶ Copy of employment contract or letter from company confirming salary and appointment.

▶ Character references – one or two will suffice, preferably from an Australian work colleague, etc. This is obviously hard if you've just relocated. One from your UK landlord or employer would help if this is all that is available.

▶ Proof of Australian bank account.

I was in an unhappy scenario where an agent was trying to extend a tenancy term and increase my offer above the advertised rate to provide assurance that I was 'in the running'. Come to think of it, I've had terrible experiences in most of my interactions with real-estate agents, but don't let that impair your judgement. It really depends on your circumstances, the agent involved, and how popular the property is.

Looking for a property a few weeks either side of Christmas can be angst inducing. Much of the property market will slow down with viewings stopping a week or two beforehand, and the market doesn't wake up again until the end of January. Short-term accommodation and hotels are notoriously busy during this period also – it is the double whammy of Christmas and the major summer holidays all in one.

BUYING A PROPERTY

The property market in Australia is buoyant, especially in urban areas. Owning your own property is considered the Aussie dream and is a common aspiration. According to the Australian Bureau of Statistics (ABS), around 70% of Aussies own a property.

Most properties available for sale are listed on the usual suspects: www.domain.com.au or www.realestate.com.au.

Auctions are a common way of selling, or attempting to sell, property in Australia. Again, this varies by state. Whilst properties may not always sell at auction, it is a popular strategy, as it creates a deadline for both the seller and buyer and will quite often encourage action and a decision around the set timeframe.

Permanent residents are able to buy property and have the same entitlements to government rebates and grants as citizens. These vary widely by state and are subject to constant change. If you are serious about buying property, it is best to seek counsel with a lawyer, conveyancer, or buyer's agent.

Temporary residents (i.e. 457 visa holders) must seek approval from the Foreign Investment Review Board before any property purchase. Visit www.firb.gov.au for more information.

FURNISHING YOUR HOME

Waiting for your shipment can take a number of weeks and a lot of patience. You may need to rent some furniture to keep you going in the interim.

Sydney, Melbourne, and Brisbane are well catered for in this regard, with a few companies offering 'starter' packages which include the basics of what you need:

www.pabs.com.au
www.livingedgerental.com.au
www.valiant.com.au
www.mrrental.com.au
www.allaboutrental.com.au – Perth only
www.bestrentals.com.au – Perth only
www.argusfurniturerentals.com.au – Adelaide only

If you have planned to start afresh, I cover where you might like to consider buying furniture in Step 6.

UTILITIES

Setting up utilities takes time, although there are a few tips on how to make the process more efficient. There are sites that help to consolidate the process and where you can set up all of your utilities in a few minutes:

www.directconnect.com.au
www.connectnow.com.au
www.onthemove.com.au

You can use an independent comparison site such as www.iselect. com.au to help with pricing and options for your area.

I would strongly advise that as many utilities as possible are in joint names. This can benefit the credit rating for a spouse who may not be working and helps when building local identification documents. As much as possible, all adults must be on as many 'radars' as possible to begin building a local history.

ELECTRICITY AND GAS

For electricity, all states with the exception of Western Australia, Tasmania, and Northern Territory have deregulated systems where you can choose your own electricity supplier. This is much the same with gas. Note that not all properties have gas, even in some established urban areas. If a line runs in your area (but not to your home), it is possible to get a connection for an installation fee.

COUNCIL TAX

In the case of rented properties, council tax should always be included in the rental charge. If you purchase a property, the council will be notified as part of the buying process and will send notifications to you accordingly.

Council tax rates will vary by state and by council. Each council determines the exact way the tax is calculated; it is loosely based on the value of the land.

PHONES AND BROADBAND

Telecoms are deregulated in Australia. The core players are Telstra (equivalent to BT) and Optus. Broadband options will vary by area, so, once you have an address, you can explore pricing and options with a number of suppliers. Note that setup may take a few days, even up to a week or two.

For home phone and broadband, there is a plethora of companies offering line rental, packages, and deals. These will combine a number of calls with a monthly download allowance. Depending on your area, you may have an ADSL or cable service, and not all companies will service everywhere. A site like iSelect (www.iselect.com.au) will help for comparison purposes. Optus and Telstra will be the main providers here, along with a host of other companies like iinet, TPG, Dodo, etc., depending on your state and area.

The National Broadband Network is a much-publicised government initiative which aims to roll out a lightning-fast broadband service to the whole of Australia. Given the remoteness of much of the country, this is an ambitious objective, and a project which will continue for a number of years to come.

From a mobile perspective, you will recognise names such as Virgin and Vodafone from the UK, in addition to Telstra and Optus. Mobile phone contract applications will request an income level. Most who do not draw an income can easily start using 'Pay as You Go', called 'Prepay/Prepaid' here, until a credit rating is built. Keeping (porting) your phone number is straightforward if you decide to set up on a contract or move to another network.

STRATA (MAINTENANCE) FEES

Strata fees cover the costs of maintenance of common property. Rental properties will have this included as part of the weekly rent. Property owners must pay these, usually in relation to the size of their private property as a portion of the whole building or land. Depending on the level of amenities and properties on a site, this can vary significantly. The strata fee is often listed along with the property price.

WATER BILLS

Water bills for a rental property are sometimes paid for by the owner and included in the rental – check with the rental agent. Some will send you a bill at the end of each quarter for your contribution to the water usage.

If you own your property, this will, of course, be your responsibility. On your bill, you can expect a flat service charge and a usage charge based on the metered amount you have used for the billing period.

PAYING BILLS

A necessary chore, utilities and other companies provide a number of standard options for payment – credit card, at the post office, over the phone, and direct debit.

There are a couple of additional ways that exist in Australia – not considerably easier but, nonetheless, a common way to pay.

When online banking, one option is 'BPay', allowing you to pay direct from your bank account. If available as a payment option, your bill will state a biller code and what number (usually your account number) to use as a reference for your payment transaction. These numbers will remain in your records for future bill payments.

'Postbillpay' offers the option to pay via the internet through the post office and with your credit card. This is basically an online alternative to showing up in person. Learn more at www.postbillpay.com.au.

Earning an income

EMPLOYMENT IN AUSTRALIA

There is a buoyant economy in Australia. Even with the recent global financial crisis, unemployment has, relative to the rest of the Western world, been low. There is, however, a general caution in the economy, with fewer people moving jobs and employers taking additional care with appointments.

Ensure that your CV (commonly called résumé here) is updated with your most relevant work experience first, with all time gaps accounted for. It is best to keep this as succinct as possible, around two to three pages as a guideline; ensure the layout is clean and easy to read. Be sure to include your visa status or whatever entitles you to work here legally – either as a permanent resident or if you are a named spouse on a temporary work visa. You will also need a Tax File Number (TFN); more on this in Step 4.

Note that, for the purpose of verifying your skills to work in your chosen profession for your visa (refer to Step 1), your CV may need to be very detailed and much longer than for job applications.

Finding work in Australia can be challenging. It is a smaller market simply due to the relatively small population that is dispersed over a vast country. There is a seemingly disproportionate number of recruiters managing placements. Senior positions, work in sales, and roles requiring 'softer' skills are tough to break into without an established network of contacts and local experience. Of course, overseas experience is respected and in many cases revered. However, in many industries, it is perceived that the Australian market is different and special, thus requiring local knowledge and expertise. This can be frustrating to start with, so you must persevere and stay positive. This is not to say your task is impossible – it can simply take time and patience to find the right role.

The best advice is to start researching your industry and market as soon as you know you will be coming to Australia. If you have any links or contacts, it is highly recommended you explore them. No matter how tenuous the link may be, it is always worth having a conversation or introduction. You will generally get a helpful or at least friendly response that may be able to point you in the right direction. Many jobs are not advertised (estimated at around 70%), with employers relying on networking, recruiters, and word of mouth. Australia can be a surprisingly small place, and you never know who knows who and where that may lead. Most jobs that are advertised will appear online, as well as in industry journals and websites, along with the weekend newspapers. The best websites to start with are www.seek.com.au or www.mycareer.com.au.

Recruiters can be found in the directories on the above websites and would be a good place to start when working out who best to send your CV to. International recruiters such as Michael Page and Hudson and Hays have a decent presence here, so if you have any existing relationships in the UK, an introduction or mention of a name would not go amiss. Prior contacts and networks should be explored as much as possible – helping to ensure you cover any roles that may not be advertised.

Once you receive a job offer, look out for the salary and ensure you are clear on whether it includes or excludes the compulsory pension contribution (called 'super', short for superannuation). By law, this is currently 9.25% and can therefore make a substantial difference to the overall package.

Some useful employment contract terms are below. You can obtain additional information from Fairwork Australia at www.fairwork.gov.au.

▶ Probation period – this is an opportunity at the start of your employment for both you or your employer to terminate the contract for any reason. Depending on the circumstances, this can range from one to six months. The standard for a full-time role is usually three months.

▶ Notice period – this is the period the employer or employee must give as notice before employment can be terminated. This is generally one month once the probation period has passed; it can be more or less depending on the role and circumstances.

▶ Salary sacrifice/packaging – this varies according to circumstances and the specific arrangement. Generally, it is a benefit in exchange for the monetary value/salary, thus, the employee has a lower taxable income.

▶ Novated car lease – usually part of a salary sacrifice arrangement, the cost of a car lease can be deducted by the employer from the employee's pre-tax income.

▶ Parental leave – by law, employees who have served 12 months continuously with their employer are permitted to take leave when a new child is born or adopted. Either parent can be considered the primary carer and is entitled to 18 weeks' parental leave pay if their individual taxable income is less than AU$150,000. The employer is obliged to hold their job, or a similar role, open, at the same salary level for 12 months. The secondary carer is entitled to two weeks' pay at the minimum wage for leave taken to spend time with the new arrival. Employers, of course, have their own benefit policies so may offer more than the legal requirement: in paid allowance, the number of months a job will be held open to await the return of the employee, allowance for the secondary carer, and so on. This is currently a hot topic in Australia as the legal minimum is low in relation to some countries. It is subject to change and variance, depending on the employer. For more information on this, visit www.humanservices.gov.au.

▶ Annual leave – the legal minimum for those in full-time employment is 20 days. In general terms, employees can take their leave when reasonable and agreed with their employer. Note that many corporates will shut down for a period over Christmas and New Year ('Annual Shut Down'), and can direct employees to take this time from their annual leave allowance. This can be complicated, as paid leave is accrued in Australia and can't be taken unless it is 'banked up'. Many industries and jobs are subject to different minimum conditions and varying rulings may apply. It is, therefore, best to check with Fair Work Australia in conjunction with your employer on this one.

▶ Long service leave – this is paid leave which can be taken after ten years' continuous service with one employer. Essentially a short sabbatical, this can vary by state and is usually around eight weeks in duration.

▶ Flexible working – a hot topic of the past few years, some employers offer options such as working from home or flexibility with office/working hours. This is generally subject to the employer's discretion, length of tenure, and other personal circumstances.

- Personal/carer's leave – this is essentially sick leave and can be used for oneself, or to care for an immediate family member who is sick or has an unexpected emergency. For those in full-time employment, the paid legal entitlement is ten days per year. This is normally pro rata for those working part-time.

SETTING UP A BUSINESS IN AUSTRALIA

Australia is a unique country in many ways. The people, geography, and demand here can vary greatly from many other Western markets, despite illusions of it being 'similar' to the UK. The market in Australia can differ immensely. It is essential to conduct due diligence and ensure the viability of any product or service. What may work in the UK may simply not have a population to sustain it or the same appetite to make it appealing and saleable here in Australia. Tastes, preferences, and resource availability all make for a subtly different market, so do investigate this should you consider setting up your own enterprise.

Having said all of this, Australia has a bright entrepreneurial scene and a vibrant business community. Many women, especially, are escaping corporate careers to seek better work-life balance and spend more time with their children. Social trends in flexible working and people seeking better work-life balance are driving this change, along with online capabilities giving access to a global marketplace.

Starting a business in any country requires compliance and a strong personal constitution. Compliance and obligations in Australia can be complex, depending on the size of a business, and business taxation tends to be high. Considerations such as the number of staff you employ, licences and registrations required to operate, premises, and securing any assets all must be taken with care.

There are government resources and business networking communities and forums which can help. The best advice, however, will come from a good accountant who can help with how to structure your business, budgeting and setup, and the all-important tax obligations.

The government website www.business.gov.au is a great place to start. This government initiative helps provide businesses with critical information in an easy-to-understand format in a central location.

Note that workplace laws and regulations when you employ staff are stringent – minimum wage, leave entitlements, insurances, and sick cover will vary considerably from the UK. Not to mention the considerably different terminologies that can flummox the most astute of entrepreneurs! Information can be sought from the Fair Work Ombudsman: www.fairwork.gov.au.

Education and childcare

CHILDCARE AND BABYSITTING

Childcare professionals and centres must be licenced in Australia. A variety of childcare services are available, ranging from day-care centres to nannies and au pairs. Many schools will also offer after-school care.

A good place to start when considering your options is www.mychild.gov.au.

There is also the highly-sought-after option of 'Family Day Care'. This is a home-based facility where the childcare educator looks after a smaller number of children in their own home: www.familydaycare.com.au.

Federal financial assistance through the Australian government is available to those who are eligible. The requirements are constantly changing. The 'Child Care Rebate' (CCR) is not income tested, but the 'Child Care Benefit' is income dependent and is only available to PRs and citizens.

There is a plethora of eligibility factors. For up-to-date information, it's best to visit both of these links to see how your circumstances marry up to the requirements:

www.humanservices.gov.au/customer/services/centrelink/child-care-rebate

www.humanservices.gov.au/customer/services/centrelink/child-care-benefit

A host of websites and agencies exist to match babysitters and nannies with families; more on this in Step 6. There is also the option of advertising for yourself on websites such as www.gumtree.com.au or Seek, one of the largest job posting websites: www.seek.com.au.

SCHOOLING AND EDUCATION

Schooling and education guidelines in Australia vary slightly by state. There are both public (state) and private options. Schools in each sector can be single faith, non-denominational, arts, or sports focused – most needs are comfortably catered for here. The vast majority of schools will have a compulsory school uniform, all of which will include a hat and a policy around sun protection. This is government mandated, and it's a case of 'no hat, no play'!

School years and respective ages are similar to the UK. However, do note that there are slight differences by state. Ensure that you check the specific age cut-offs for your future home state (web links can be found later in this section). Here is an overview:

Pre-school and kindergarten
Pre-school: 4 to 5-year-olds
Kindergarten: 5 to 6-year-olds

Primary school
Year 1: 6 to 7-year-olds
Year 2: 7 to 8-year-olds
Year 3: 8 to 9-year-olds
Year 4: 9 to 10-year-olds
Year 5: 10 to 11-year-olds
Year 6: 11 to 12-year-olds
Year 7: 12 to 13-year-olds

Secondary / High school
Year 7: 12 to 13-year-olds
Year 8: 13 to 14-year-olds

Year 9: 14 to 15-year-olds

Year 10: 15 to 16-year-olds

Year 11: 16 to 17-year-olds Higher School Certificate (HSC)

Year 12: 17 to 18-year-olds Higher School Certificate (HSC)

INTERNATIONAL BACCALAUREATE (IB)

An internationally recognised curriculum – many private and some public schools offer this standard: www.ibo.org

NAPLAN

Naplan is a compulsory testing of numeracy and literacy in years three, five, seven, and nine: www.nap.edu.au.

This system and testing serves as an independent performance benchmark for all schools, public and private, in Australia. Performance tables for all schools can be found on the website and can help in guiding or confirming a decision on where you may choose to enrol your offspring.

For school research and comparison, there is a government website that serves to profile all schools in Australia, providing a useful central point to start your research. Here you can find comparisons for every school in Australia, whether public or private: www.myschool.edu.au.

SCHOOLS – GOVERNMENT/STATE/PUBLIC-FUNDED

Schools in highly populated areas will each have designated catchment areas. The postcode will determine eligibility and a school's obligation for your child to be enrolled. Many urban schools are over-subscribed and will go so far as to insist on proof of address (usually a rental agreement or multiple utility bills) before the enrolment procedure can actually take place.

Whilst public schools are generally 'free', there will be a small annual fee payable to cover some activities and other costs.

Here are the state system websites outlining the policies, term dates, and guidelines for the state in which you reside:

NSW: www.schools.nsw.edu.au
QLD: education.qld.gov.au
SA: www.decd.sa.gov.au
VIC: www.education.vic.gov.au
WA: www.det.wa.edu.au

Note that each state differs in terms of whether temporary residents (generally on a 457 visa) are entitled to access the public-school system for free. Fees may be payable for your child in states such as NSW, for example, with others like WA making plans to charge fees in future. Be prepared to be asked for your visa and residency status at this point.

SCHOOLS – PRIVATE/INDEPENDENT

There is a plethora of private schools in Australia. You can search by Naplan results and there are also league tables published each year.

A useful resource is www.privateschoolsdirectory.com.au.

TERM TIME AND HOLIDAYS

The school year runs according to the calendar year, making it slightly tricky when moving from the UK system. Schools generally end their school year a week or so before Christmas and return from the summer holiday immediately after the Australia Day Holiday at the very end of January.

http://australia.gov.au/topics/australian-facts-and-figures/public-holidays

State public holidays are also days off school – many of which tie in with holiday dates. Terms dates for private schools are generally shorter, offering a week or so longer per holiday period, and are individual to the school.

THE SCHOOL RUN

Note that many urban schools will not offer a school transport system. Many parents choose to do the school run themselves or will rely on public transport. This will vary according to the school and where you live. Some private schools may offer transport on a set route or collection points. Do check on this when registering your child and choosing where to live.

Getting around

Driving is a common choice here. Overall, there is nearly one car per adult of driving age, according to the government's ABS website (abs.gov.au). This will, of course, vary according to remoteness, income, and a heap of other factors, but, in short, most people prefer to have a car.

CYCLING

Australia is a relatively eco-conscious nation. As a result, cities are constantly increasing their cycle-path networks and are actively promoting the use of bicycles as a viable means of transport. Cycling is gaining in popularity in all cities. Many offices are set up with shower facilities for staff who choose to bike to work.

PARKING

Parking is limited in all metro areas. Sydney is a main culprit here, given the size of the population and it being a major commercial centre. Parking in Sydney can be astronomically expensive, so many will choose to use the public transport network to commute to work. Melbourne suffers similarly but has a very good tram system supported by buses.

Those with disabilities are well catered for in most cases, and parents with young children will usually find a selection of designated parking spots in most shopping centres, with roomier spaces and closer proximity to entrances.

PUBLIC TRANSPORT

Public transport networks are, overall, fairly reliable in Australia. Much is dependent on the nuances of a particular route, journey time, and variables such as traffic and maintenance. Different modes are available also – with buses, trams, and trains being supported in some cities by a ferry system. Underground networks do not really exist here, but main-line trains do have sections of underground tracks and stations in urban areas. Whilst the different modes exist and are relatively well connected, the integration of the fares and pricing has much catching up to do. A new electronic ticketing system called Opal is being tested in Sydney as I write, and the 'myki' system has been very recently implemented in Melbourne to mixed reviews.

All five capital cities have a free bus service of sorts. These cater more for visitors and are mostly restricted to a small loop or stretch of the CBD area.

Where you live may be dependent on public transport, and Google Maps is a great resource for spotting whether a bus route runs through an area, or if there is a train or tram line that passes through.

Increasingly, most buses and trams require the fare to be purchased in advance. Be sure to check this with your local network so you are prepared for your journey.

You can look further into the state and city public transport offerings via these links:

NSW: www.131500.com.au
QLD: translink.com.au
SA: www.adelaidemetro.com.au
VIC: ptv.vic.gov.au
WA: www.transperth.wa.gov.au

RENTING A CAR

Car rental is a fairly simple process in Australia. Most cities have a wide network of both global and local players. You will recognise the likes of Hertz, Avis, and Budget, but it's worth looking into independent players who may be cheaper. Always ask what your damage liability is when you are hiring a car, as insurance coverage does vary by company. Note that renting a car at any airport will be subject to a tax or fee for the convenience. Some companies (mostly the independent ones) will offer a shuttle service that will take you away from the airport terminal to avoid this. You will likely wish to research and arrange this beforehand, as the shuttles may not cater for speculative customer pick-ups.

TAXIS

Taxis/cabs are a popular choice and reasonably priced in relation to Europe. Each city has a few taxi companies licenced to serve the area. Some of the usual protocol for taxis will be no different to what you are used to. Typically, all taxis:

- ▶ Are metered.

- ▶ Can be reached by dialling 131 008, which diverts to the prominent taxi company in that city.

- ▶ Put their light on when available; light off when occupied or unavailable.

- ▶ Have a flag fall (starting) fare, which will vary by city/state.

- ▶ Will be required to have the driver's photo ID on display.

- ▶ Must be licenced to carry passengers.

- ▶ Can be flagged down and stop almost anywhere.

- ▶ Will charge a booking fee.

- ▶ Must have their fare information on clear display.

► There are a portion of taxis that cater for disabled and wheelchair access, and a 'MaxiTaxi' allows for a larger number of passengers.

A word of warning - taxis are not obliged to meet a booking if unavailable. A 'booking' is not guaranteed and will simply be put to the network for a driver to accept, or not, as the case may be.

Chapter re-cap –
a place called home...

+ Your arrival will be exciting, disorientating, and the race is on to find somewhere to live. Finding a home and a routine is the beginning of your life in Australia.

+ Research into areas and amenities is important to determine what lifestyle you can expect, and what your daily life will look like.

+ Looking for a home can be hard work with the new terminologies and the different way that the rental market works here.

>>

+ Going back to basics is a matter of getting organised, and you'll be surprised at how much is involved with setting up from scratch.

+ It's time to establish your ideal routine; find schools, jobs, and your commute; set up your new home; understand how things work; and explore your new surroundings.

+ You might be a bit shellshocked at this stage in the process. It's mentally and physically draining for the first few weeks as you find your bearings. Once you're set up in your new home, your focus will turn to feeling at home as quickly as possible.

STEP 4

TACKLE THE NECESSITIES

This step is crucial, because, once you have done everything in this phase, you are compliant and will have more of a sense of belonging. These are the registrations, tasks, and paperwork that you will have had for as long as you can remember back home and perhaps even take for granted. You will likely not have thought twice about how these things work in the UK, and not knowing the ropes here may make you feel like an outsider. Your departure from the UK will likely have wiped much of the slate clean, or at least put things on hold. It is crucial to handle these necessities as soon as you can to build your identity here.

I would use this section first and foremost as a reference guide. Whilst necessary, this step is quite mundane and boring, so please bear with me.

The order in which you carry out these tasks is not crucial and depends on your circumstances. I would suggest that, for most, getting finance and health matters in check would be a priority.

100 point identification

Most of what you will need to do will require 100 points of identification. This is a selection of documents that prove your identity and help to prevent fraud. Each document of proof is allocated points, and you need 100 to open bank and Medicare accounts or register for a driver's licence, for example.

You can only have one primary document, such as a birth certificate or passport, worth 70 points. Secondary documents must be photo ID to get you, for example, a further 40 points. However, this is a chicken-and-egg situation, as other documents that are permitted include council rates notices, credit cards, and utility bills, which require you to be set up already!

Here is a listing that will help give you an idea, based on the paperwork you are likely to have with you. Note that this is subject to change, so check online with the institution you are registering with:

- ▶ Primary documents, only one of these permitted (70 points)
    - ▽ Birth certificate
    - ▽ Citizenship certificate
    - ▽ Current passport

- Secondary documents, must have photo and name (40 points)
  - ▽ Driver's licence issued by an Australian State or Territory
  - ▽ An identification card issued to a student at a tertiary education institution

Name and signature (25 points)

- ▽ Credit card
- ▽ Foreign driver's licence
- ▽ Medicare card (signature not required on Medicare card)
- ▽ EFTPOS (bank) card

Name and address (25 points)

- ▽ Records of a public utility – phone, water, gas, or electricity bill
- ▽ Records of a financial institution
- ▽ Lease/rental agreement
- ▽ Rent receipt from a licenced real-estate agent

Name and date of birth (25 points)

- ▽ Record of a primary, secondary, or tertiary education institution attended within the last ten years
- ▽ Record of professional or trade association of which you are a member

Banks, credit cards, and money

A priority will be to set up an Australian bank account. This can be done prior to leaving the UK or on arrival in Australia. You will need 100 points of identification to verify who you are.

There are four major banks in Australia – Westpac, ANZ, NAB, and Commonwealth Bank (CBA). The wider market includes HSBC and some regional banks such as Suncorp, Bendigo, Bank West, and Bank of Queensland (BOQ).

Many bank accounts are subject to a monthly fee and/or limitations in terms of number of transactions/withdrawals. Credit cards also attract fees, some relatively high – so it's best to shop around. Most credit cards give the option to collect loyalty points – some have their own schemes, others are aligned with frequent-flyer schemes. Again, it's best to shop around for the best deal and arrangement for your circumstances.

Obtaining a credit card without an income is tricky. Once a regular salary is evident, you're more likely to get your application approved.

Most banks will offer a set of two linked credit cards – typically American Express along with Mastercard or Visa. This normally helps as a great number of vendors do not accept AmEx, or will charge a premium to do so. It is not uncommon, in fact, for vendors to charge for the privilege of using 'EFTPOS' (or at least have a minimum transaction amount to allow card use). EFTPOS is any transaction using a card and electronic point of sale system.

You will, of course, receive a debit card (ask for a credit/debit card if you're eligible) for use in shops and at ATMs. Unlike in the UK, you cannot use the debit facility as with Switch for online shopping – hence, a combined credit/debit card is useful to serve this purpose without some of the fees associated with credit card payments.

If you have more than one bank account (e.g. current account and a savings account), you will be asked to allocate one as your 'savings' and one as your 'cheque' account for ATM (cash machine) and EFTPOS purposes. This is VERY confusing but will become clear when you go shopping, where the checkout assistant will ask you whether you'd like the payment to come from 'cheque, savings, or credit' account. If you're using a credit card, respond with credit. Use of your debit card will mean you need to make a choice.

Cash is a standard payment method (except, oddly, for no-frills airlines who only accept credit cards when paying for sundries on board). Cheques are hardly used at all, although you will receive a cheque book as standard when you open a bank account.

Interest rates in Australia are set by the Reserve Bank of Australia (RBA). They are reviewed and announced 11 months of the year, on the first Tuesday of the month. January is the month in which much of Australia goes on holiday, as it ties in the Christmas and big summer holidays, and the RBA has January as a holiday too.

Banks set their own savings and mortgage rates which are tied to, but mostly higher than, the RBA rates.

MOVING MONEY FROM THE UK

There are various ways to move money from one country to another. Most will assume that to make an international transfer is the easiest way. Whilst it's convenient, it will incur high fees and a less than competitive exchange rate.

If you open an Australian bank account from the UK, you can likely arrange to have your Sterling deposited into a holding account for transfer when you want to leave or a later date, in the event you wish to wait for a change in the exchange rate.

The other option is to register for a foreign exchange broker. The exchange rate will vary according to the amount you'd like to transfer. This method requires another application and party but can save you money in the long term. Once registered, the process involves locking in an agreed exchange rate and transferring the money to be converted into a nominated bank account, before the purchased currency is transferred into the bank account of your choice.

TAX AND COMPLIANCE

Australia has a progressive and complex tax system. The more you earn, the more you pay. No source of income is exempt. Everyone drawing an income requires a Tax File Number (TFN) – it is a unique identifier to you, in relation to your earnings. This is similar to the National Insurance (NI) number in the UK.

Visit www.ato.gov.au to register for a TFN and for more details on tax compliance. You will need the usual 100 points of identification, and the TFN application can be completed online or in person at an ATO office. You will receive your unique number in the mail once processed.

Everyone who receives an income, in whatever form, must file a tax return every year. The tax year runs from July 1–June 30 every year, and the equivalent here of the HM Revenue & Customs is the Australian Tax Office (ATO). Most who are unfamiliar with accounts will have a qualified accountant or bookkeeper that can help with this process and file the return electronically on your behalf.

Tax is a complex issue in any country. For further information relating to your specific circumstances, I recommend that you approach an accountant as soon as any question or uncertainty arises.

Sales tax is referred to as GST – Goods and Services Tax – and at time of writing is 10%. The norm is for most prices in retail shops to include GST. However, do look out for this, as some pricing (such as services) will have GST on top of the price quoted. Most food items not considered a 'luxury' that are purchased from a grocery store or supermarket are not subject to GST. Food served to you in a restaurant or café, however, is subject to GST.

All income earners must pay a Medicare Levy and surcharges but may be eligible for certain rebates. This is income tested in line with tiered thresholds. People who choose to have medical insurance receive a reduced premium, contributed to by the government.

Driving in Australia

Car ownership and driving are very common in Australia. Like in the UK, we drive on the left in a right-hand-drive vehicle. Note that most cars here have an automatic transmission rather than the usual manual transmission.

The main car brands you recognise from Europe are available here in Australia. Japanese and locally-produced cars are popular due to their more affordable pricing. Cars are taxed very highly here, so be prepared to see considerably higher prices, even with the currency conversion. A brand new basic model VW Golf, for example, would have a starting price of around AU$25,000, or a locally popular Japanese car such as a Toyota Corolla would start at around AU$20,000.

BUYING A CAR

Most people, in even the most urban of areas, will choose to buy a car. You can opt to go to a car dealership to get relevant warranties and peace of mind with your purchase. As in the UK, car dealerships will manage sales for certain manufacturers. Alternatively, you can start by visiting these websites, which are aggregated new and used car sales databases. Just enter your postcode and other parameters, and away you go:

www.carsales.com.au
www.drive.com.au

If you are interested in making an offer, don't be afraid to negotiate or haggle on the car's advertised price. If you are opting to finance the car, there is usually scope for negotiation here, too. Other added extras such as car accessories, window tinting (a necessity with the harsh sun, in my opinion), extended warranties, a free tank of petrol – throw all of these into the pot as a basis for your price discussion.

Buying and running a car involves the usual plethora of paperwork and compliance. If you purchase a car from a dealer, most of this will be handled for you. If you buy privately, ensure that you have all of the following taken care of.

Refer to the relevant transport body in your state for detailed information:

NSW – www.rms.nsw.gov.au
QLD – www.tmr.qld.gov.au
SA – www.sa.gov.au

VIC – www.vicroads.vic.gov.au

WA – www.transport.wa.gov.au

- ▶ Stamp duty and other government charges – when buying a car, ask for the 'Drive Away' price which will include all of these supplements.

- ▶ Car registration (licence plate, called 'rego').

- ▶ Compulsory Third Party insurance (CTP) – this varies by state and is also referred to as a 'Green Slip'. As its name suggests, this a legal requirement and covers claims for third party personal injury rather than the car itself. You cannot register your car (get your rego) until you have purchased CTP.

- ▶ Pink Slip – vehicles more than five years old need this annual inspection before car registration can be renewed. This is the same principle as the MOT in the UK. Similar to the UK, car repair garages need to be approved to offer this and will send the approval online and direct to the transport authority for your state.

- ▶ Third party insurance or comprehensive insurance – as in the UK, there are varying levels of insurance available depending on your budget.

- ▶ A driving licence is, of course, a key factor to driving legally in Australia. Licences must have photo ID.

OTHER HINTS AND TIPS IN RELATION TO DRIVING:

- ▶ Visit your transport authority website and familiarise yourself with road signs – many are different from the UK, and this will help with your driving confidence.

- Drink–drive laws are strict in Australia, and speed limits are strictly enforced, with heavy fines and point penalties (called 'demerits') if they are broken.

- Park in the direction of the traffic.

- Carry your licence with you at all times – it's a legal requirement.

- Seatbelts are compulsory for all passengers.

- Using or even touching your mobile phone is illegal whilst your car is moving or not parked, and you can receive an on-the-spot fine for breaking this law. Use of your phone must be entirely hands-free.

- Approved child or booster seats/restraints are compulsory for all children under seven years. Babies under six months must be rearward facing. Check with your transport authority for detailed information.

- During public holiday periods, most states will enforce a 'double demerits' period. This means that speeding or any other offence will carry double the usual penalty. Ignore at your peril. Losing your driver's licence was never easier.

- Throwing cigarette butts out of the window whilst driving is generally considered poor form given the high fire risk in this country.

- Fuel prices are cheaper here than in the UK but rising fast. Prices fluctuate multiple times during every week at intervals, unbeknownst to most of the public! This is driven by the gas companies, and you will notice these changes every few days. Overall, pricing tends to be higher around weekends, public holidays, and other busy periods.

- Traffic light sequence is Red-Green-Amber-Red.

TOLLS

Many states have toll roads – these are cashless and payable within a few days of passing through a toll payment area. You can, however, obtain a toll tag which can be kept in your car to be 'blipped' on passing, and some states also have casual arrangements whereby your licence plate is registered for a time period and you are billed for use accordingly.

You can drive interstate with your toll tag, and your account is debited as required. Toll accounts are usually automatically 'topped up' with a nominated value according to your frequency of use.

GETTING YOUR AUSTRALIAN DRIVING LICENCE

If you are a temporary resident (on a 457 visa), you are not required to have an Australian licence if you have a valid UK driving licence. If you are a permanent resident, you have a three-month grace period to drive using your UK licence. I would suggest this is one of the first things you organise, as it's a very useful piece of identification. Generally, it's a matter of queuing, applying, sitting for a photo, paying, and you have your licence replaced. It's not usually necessary to have a practical or knowledge test. Note that your UK licence will be voided as part of this process. A driver's licence is a useful form of ID that can help to get to your 100 points needed for many applications and registrations. You will, however, need proof of an address.

As with all regulations, they are subject to change, so it's best to check with the transport authority in your home state. It's also worth checking in advance what documents you will need and the process they use for issuing licences.

Generally, you will need to bring:

- ► Proof of identity and your permanent residency status
- ► Proof of address
- ► Method of payment – credit cards are fine

Health matters

Medicare is the government healthcare system in Australia. Residents eligible for a Medicare card can access the subsidised medications and treatment available from healthcare providers. UK citizens are eligible to access Medicare rebates as the UK has a reciprocal agreement with Australia.

It is essential that you find a general practitioner (GP) as soon as possible once you arrive in the country. With the exception of emergencies, where you should go to a hospital emergency section, your GP will be your first point of contact for all health-related issues and will refer and recommend if specialist expertise is required.

FIND A DOCTOR

You can choose where to be treated, and some will travel far and wide to see a preferred doctor. You will need to show your Medicare card. The best place to start (in the absence of a good referral) is a medical directory, good ol' Yellow Pages, or an internet search for your area:

www.doctors.com.au
www.yellowpages.com.au

You may notice some doctors' surgeries (or opticians for that matter) advertising that they offer 'bulk billing'. This essentially means that their fee will not be more than the government rebate, so your visit will not cost you anything 'out of pocket'. The doctor will then claim for all of the patient treatments in a bulk bill to Medicare. Medicare is a government subsidised health system where set rebates apply to each treatment according to its code. These are generally reviewed every year and may vary slightly in line with inflation and other variables.

For example, the standard Medicare rebate/refund for a standard doctor's consultation is $36.30. My Doctor chooses to charge $80 for this appointment, which I will duly pay direct to the surgery. The rebate can be placed directly into my bank account (as long as they have my information), or I go to a Medicare office to make the claim and will receive the $36.30 in cash. Therefore, the appointment cost me the difference (the 'out of pocket' or 'gap' expense), $43.70.

Prescriptions given to you by a doctor can be fulfilled at a pharmacy. Most medications are subsidised by Medicare, but note that the pharmacy can set whatever price they like. There are no set prescription charges. It pays to shop around for certain medications – I have inadvertently paid more than twice the price for some medications before becoming savvier about where to shop. There are many discount pharmacies and chains like The Chemist Warehouse which will offer bargain basement prices for an identical product.

The pharmacy will often ask you if you would like the branded medication or the 'generic' version, which is cheaper. For ongoing and repeat prescriptions, you will have a set number of 'repeats' stipulated on the script, which is in addition to the prescription.

E.g. a prescription for six months, requiring one box monthly, will have 'five repeats' marked on the script.

FIND A VET

Much like when finding a doctor, you can use an internet search, directory, or Yellow Pages if you don't have the benefit of a personal recommendation. Vet expenses can be high, so many pet owners choose to have pet insurance coverage. Whilst, like all insurance, there are different levels of cover and excess payable, it can really take the sting out of the cost for unexpected bills. Once again, it's always a good idea to shop around for the deal that best meets your needs and circumstances.

MEDICARE REGISTRATION

Registering for Medicare is straightforward but can take time. You need to visit a Medicare office with relevant documents and, subject to providing the necessary information, will be issued a temporary card on the spot. Families and married or de facto couples are usually registered with the same card and number.

Find your nearest Medicare office by visiting: humanservices.findnearest.com.au

I would strongly suggest that you check on arrival to confirm what you should bring with you dependent on your circumstances. Where it can get tricky is if an applicant does not have the right to work, so it then becomes necessary to prove the relationship that entitles you to be in Australia. This will vary according to your circumstances, so do check before making the trip.

In general terms, you will need:

- ▶ Completed enrolment form – available via www.humanservices.gov.au – in the 'Forms' section
- ▶ Passport and a valid visa

MEDICAL INSURANCE

Private health insurance in Australia is an interesting concept, offering further subsidy. Note that Medicare does not cover ambulance call outs, for which callers will be charged a fee. This is generally a good reason to have health cover, and many companies will offer this limited level of cover. Overall, you will still incur out-of-pocket expenses if you require surgery, an ambulance, or certain tests. Your medical insurance serves to further reduce the amount by supplementing the Medicare rebate that you receive back for that treatment, unless you are treated as a public patient, in which case you can be treated for free, subject to waiting lists and other conditions. Note that your income tax may be subject to a surcharge if you do not have medical insurance, the thinking being that you may be a heavier burden on the health system than if you have insurance.

Health insurance will vary according to your circumstances and by health fund, so it's best to shop around. The comparison site www.iselect.com.au is a good place to start given there are many companies, and your cover will depend on the state you live in. Health insurance companies also have physical branches that you can visit. This is helpful to discuss which policy is best for your circumstances. Basic cover is just for ambulance and hospital care. Some choose to have 'extras' cover. Extras cover offers a subsidy on ancillary care, such as dental and optical. Note that most insurance companies will have a 'waiting period', so you may not be permitted to claim until the time has passed. This will be in the terms of your policy, often called a 'Product Disclosure Statement' (PDS).

Home insurance

Building insurance is, in my view, a necessity if you own your property. If you are renting, the building should be insured by the owner.

Having your contents insured is highly recommended in the event of theft or any other unfortunate incident. Again, you can use a comparison site or choose to complete your own internet search. Many companies will allow you to apply online. Note that companies will have different security and other requirements before they will insure you. This is especially true if you live in a block of units (apartments).

Most insurance requires you to pay upfront, and paying via monthly instalments will be charged at a higher fee overall. This differs by company and will generally be offered as a selling point by some who don't charge a premium for monthly payments.

Mobile phone

Being connected is crucial in your initial days of making appointments and enquiries and staying in touch with family and friends.

First port of call is a newsagents, convenience store, or phone network store where you can purchase a SIM card for your mobile and get it registered as soon as possible. You will need identification and an address to register your SIM card. Ensure that you remember the information you have registered with in order that you may update it when you have a more permanent address and arrangement here. If viable, it is a good idea to stop by a network shop run by Telstra, Optus, or Vodafone (the main networks in Australia) to understand the best-value options for your usage and circumstances.

www.optus.com.au
www.telstra.com.au
www.vodafone.com.au

The only likely option on arrival is a Prepaid arrangement, as you will unlikely have any credit rating to speak of when you first arrive. Topping up your credit is easy online or with vouchers purchased from newsagents or convenience stores.

Notification of address change

At this stage, you will have an address. The first to know about this should be your shipping company. After this, it is advisable to have your UK post directed to you unless you have a trustworthy person who can take care of this for you. Banks, HM Revenue & Customs, and other institutions should be made aware of your new whereabouts.

Pension (superannuation)

By law, it is compulsory for employers to contribute to a superannuation (retirement) fund. There is a number of set criteria as to whether you are eligible, and your entitlements may depend on your circumstances. It's best to visit the ATO government website for more information.

In terms of setup, there is a multitude of financial services companies offering superannuation, should you wish to set up your own fund. More than likely, you will be set up via your employer, who will often have a preferred company. Note that most have management fees, and the employer may have an arrangement whereby these are waived. It is possible to make higher contributions to your super fund out of your pre-tax income, which some people choose to do to keep their super topped up and to lower the tax burden. You may wish to ensure that you have income protection as an added feature just in case the worst happens and you suffer from loss of income for a period.

If you are a temporary resident (457 visa), you are able (subject to certain requirements and criteria) to withdraw and transfer your super back to the UK when you leave.

The topics of finance, tax, and super can be very complex, intertwined, and individual to your circumstances, so please seek advice according to your needs.

Pet compliance

When your pet arrives, it is important that it is registered with your local council. Pet registrations are managed on a local basis, not at state or federal level. Ensure that this is handled within a few weeks of your pet's arrival.

It is also a good idea to ensure your pet's microchip is on the Central Animal Register – this is a central database containing pet information. For more information, visit www.car.com.au.

Pet ownership is high in Australia, so finding everything you will need to keep your pet healthy is straightforward. If you are planning to bring your pet, a period of quarantine will apply, so it is advisable to seek out a local vet to ensure you can get your pet checked out and settled into their new life.

Checklist of personal registrations and setup

Bank	
Doctor	
Driving licence	
Medical insurance	
Medicare	
Mobile phone	
Tax File Number	

Chapter re-cap – **I'm a legal alien...**

+ Mundane but essential, you'll be going through the motions to get through the compliance involved in this phase.

+ Leaving the UK wipes the slate clean, so it's important to start building your identity here in Australia.

+ There's a sense that you're starting from scratch here; it will likely have been many years since you've done most of what you need to do here.

+ It's hard work getting this all done in one go, but the sooner you do, the faster you can start learning the ropes.

STEP 5

LEARN THE ROPES

This step of your move will mainly involve learning the practicalities and how to get things done with the least amount of fuss and developing a deeper insight into your new environment. You'll be getting to know how things work and starting to settle into your new home and routine. You will inevitably have to grapple with some difficult emotions as you adjust to life in Australia.

Leaving the UK will have been exhilarating and possibly upsetting. You will experience a broad spectrum of emotions in your early days – they will all be perfectly normal. This is when the honeymoon feeling might start to fade.

You'll be excited and have a sense of wanting to get stuck into things, perhaps to get settled into life as quickly and seamlessly as possible. However, not knowing the ropes will result in feelings of overwhelm and your ignorance of how things work may lead to some frustration. The simplest of tasks will seem difficult, and you will feel irritated and self-conscious. The evenings might be lonely as you reflect on the day and possibly have chats with people back in the UK, reminding you that things are just so much easier when you know how. Culture shock may lead to isolation and homesickness – and most of us have all felt like it would be so much easier just to pack it all in and go back 'home'. Again, this is natural, and getting through it will take strength and a routine with daily and weekly purpose. There are compliance activities and registrations to get done, properties to view, and, ultimately, a new city and country to explore. With a positive frame of mind and discipline, this will keep you busy and stimulated.

Things you'll miss and what no one will tell you

It almost goes without saying that you will miss family and friends. Fortunately, Skype and social media websites will help keep you connected. Once everyone gets the time difference down pat, it can be easy and reassuring to have this time for everyone to exchange news.

You will almost certainly miss 'things' about the UK – and I will hazard a guess that some or all of the following will feature in your thinking: Marks & Spencer, using the Pound Sterling, the proximity to Europe, the wider choice of shops and products available, the fact that much of the country is within driving distance, and your favourite brands. There will be a feeling of dislodgement and limbo – home (the UK) will seem perfect. The list will go on.

There will be aspects of your former life you somehow couldn't appreciate until you landed on Australian soil. This will take some getting used to and is not a reason to be alarmed.

For example, you may realise it's not easy to find a job here; arts and culture will seem thin on the ground compared to the offering in the UK and nearby Europe; the macho approach may surprise and occasionally offend; and insects, flies, and creepy crawlies can be a surprise before you get used to them. Service can be bad here; income tax is high, and so are prices; maternity leave is meagre; childcare will have waiting lists; and there is a possible risk that fire and drought will affect you firsthand. No one will think to tell you that your first Christmas in heat and sunshine is bizarre and that you'll have better chance of enjoying a turkey with all the trimmings during winter when 'Christmas in July' is commonly celebrated.

When you have these blues, it's best to think about what Australia offers that the UK can't – more sunshine, thousands of clean beaches, an active and laid-back lifestyle, etc. This list will go on, and it should feature all of the reasons you've moved here in the first place.

Practicalities

DRESS

As you would expect, leisure attire tends to be very relaxed and casual here in Australia. Thongs (aka flip-flops), shorts, t-shirts, jeans – all are common and standard.

Given the strength of the sun, hats, sunglasses, and sunscreen feature heavily and are highly recommended as part of the daily repertoire – regardless of season or number of clouds in the sky. I cannot stress enough how strong the sun here actually is. Left uncovered or unprotected when outdoors, you can develop dangerous sunburn within just a few minutes.

No matter the calibre or cost of a restaurant, the dress code tends to be very relaxed pretty much anywhere in Australia. You will not look out of place wearing tidy jeans and a t-shirt in the most salubrious of restaurants, despite perhaps feeling a little underdressed.

Workplace dress tends to be formal office-wear in most industries, particularly in the financial and professional services. UK and US workplace and some industry norms are filtering through, with some having more of a smart casual vibe or 'jeans Friday' culture.

Our 'reverse' seasons mean that following northern hemisphere fashion results in us being what could be interpreted as behind in the style stakes. But local fashion seems to have a life and creativity of its own, with Australian fashions and tastes tending to be quirky and adventurous.

ELECTRICS

Australian plugs are either two or three pin. Sockets are three-pin to allow for this. Note that travel adapter plugs will likely only have two pins, which is sufficient.

Wiring or re-wiring of any kind (plugs, wall sockets, light fittings, etc.) needs to be carried out by a licenced electrician. Any fire or accident that may ensue as a result of a non-licenced person making these changes may not be covered by insurance. This made more sense when we visited hardware stores and discovered that plugs are not easy to come by.

Most expats tend to bring sets of multi-plugs and adapters to deal with the immediate need. Then they can decide whether to take the risk changing plugs themselves in the medium to long term. Adapters are available here in most pharmacies and office equipment stores. Truth be told, I still have one or two UK plugs in my house – this is unlikely to change in a hurry!

EMERGENCY SERVICES

Police, fire, and ambulance services can be contacted by dialling 000.

Hearing or speech impaired can make a text emergency call by dialling 106.

For more information, visit www.triplezero.gov.au.

LANGUAGE

Due to the diverse range of cultures, in some areas, all over Australia, you can sometimes close your eyes and imagine you are in Italy, Asia, or Greece.

Slang is common here, and characteristic of the Aussie way is to shorten as much as possible. Afternoon becomes arvo, presentation becomes presso, avocado avo, ambulance ambo, chickens are chooks, journalists are journos, and so on. Nothing is immune to being shortened or given a slang term. It's part of the charm, and it really is like you see on *Neighbours*! Note that there are commonly used words here that are considered offensive to Brits and yet are named brands here. One example is a cheese brand, Coon. Flippant use of what we would consider an ethnic slur does happen, and it shocked me when I first heard the word 'wog' used to describe someone of Mediterranean descent. Whilst some would consider this acceptable, I prefer not to use words that I have always understood to be offensive.

In terms of lingo and abbreviated words, here are some common terms and acronyms you will hear; it's amazing how many I've adopted without realising it – and you will too. I've also included some of the terminology that differs here – and may stop you in your tracks for a few seconds until your ears are trained.

AFL/footy – Australian Football League (aka Aussie rules)

Aniseed – fennel is sometimes known as aniseed

Anzac biscuit – oat and coconut biscuit, similar to a Hob Nob

Barbie – barbecue

Bathers/swimmers/cossie – swimming costume

Bench/benchtop – kitchen counter top

Bloody oath – too right, that's certainly true

Bogan – someone who takes little pride in their looks, similar to chav perhaps

Bonzer/ripper – great, awesome

Bottle-o – bottle shop (somewhere liquor is sold), off licence

Bowser – petrol pump

Canola oil – rapeseed oil

Capsicum – pepper

Chippie – carpenter

Cobber – friend

Coldie – beer

Crook – sick, ill

Daks – trousers

Dinkum/fair dinkum – true, genuine (fair dinkum usually expressed as a question)

Doco – document or documentary

Doona – duvet

Dunny – outside toilet

Eggplant – aubergine

Entrée – starter course

Exy – expensive

Flat white coffee – similar to a latte with less milk in ratio to coffee, with less foam

G'day – hello

Galah – silly person

Grog – alcohol

Gumboots – wellies

Icy pole – frozen popsicle

Heaps – a lot

Joggers/runners – running shoes

Lamington – cube-shaped sponge cake coated in chocolate icing and covered in coconut

Larrikin – joker, prankster

Linseed – flaxseed

Lollies – sweets, candy

Long black coffee – Americano

Lounge – sofa/couch

Manchester – bed linen

Milk bar – general store which sells hot food, some deli items, and drinks

Mozzie – mosquito

Oldies – parents

Pokies – slot/fruit machines

Pot (or middy) - slightly less than half a pint of beer. Varies by state

Prezzy – present, gift

Pumpkin – squash of any kind

Rapt/stoked – happy, delighted

Rego – vehicle registration

Rental bond – security deposit for a rental property

Root – to have sex

Schooner – roughly half a pint of beer. Varies by state

Servo – petrol station

Shallots – spring/green onions (confusing as shallots are also called shallots, eschallots, or 'French shallots')

Short black coffee – espresso

Slab – case of beer

Snag – sausage

Sook – wimp, soppy

Sparky – electrician

Strata fees – fees for maintenance to common/shared property

Superannuation – pension, often shortened to 'super'

Sunnies – sunglasses

Thongs – flip flops

Tradie – tradesperson

Turps ('hit the turps') – go out on a big bender to get drunk

Unit (in relation to property) – flat, apartment

Woop-woop – in the middle of nowhere

Yakka – work

Zucchini – courgette

MEDIA

MAGAZINES

Overall, the magazine market in Australia is fairly populated considering its size. Many of the recognised global brands such as *Vogue*, *Cosmopolitan*, and *Top Gear* are available here, as are many UK and US published magazines, albeit at a considerable price premium. You can, of course, purchase magazines at news agencies, petrol stations, and supermarkets. In many cases, it is possible to make considerable savings if you subscribe to magazines and have them delivered to your door. A visit to www.magshop.com.au is the best bet; it is a central portal for all magazines you could ever need, offering an efficient service.

NEWSPAPERS AND NEWS

The Australian media market is relatively consolidated and small in relation to most other markets.

Newspapers are predominantly run by two companies – Fairfax and News Corporation. The sheer size of Australia means there are only two national daily newspapers. The remaining key publications are regionally branded and distributed. Although, note that content that is non-region specific will be likely be syndicated, especially via the online portals.

In general, the quality of journalism is not as high as in the UK. It does, however, focus mostly on topical news and politics. The bulk of gossip, celebrity news, and popular press is left to many of the weekly magazines.

At the time of writing, *The Guardian* newspaper now has an Australian site, with the *Daily Mail* recently announcing that it will follow suit. There are also rumours that the likes of the *Huffington Post* will soon offer Australian specific content through a local domain.

National
- ▶ The Australian www.theaustralian.com.au
- ▶ The Australian Financial Review www.afr.com

Adelaide
- ▶ The Advertiser, Sunday Mail www.adelaidenow.com.au

Brisbane
- ▶ Courier Mail www.couriermail.com.au
- ▶ Brisbane Times www.brisbanetimes.com.au

Melbourne
- ▶ The Age, The Sunday Age www.theage.com.au
- ▶ The Herald Sun www.heraldsun.com.au

Perth
- ▶ The West Australian au.news.yahoo.com/thewest
- ▶ The Sunday Times www.perthnow.com.au
- ▶ WA Today www.watoday.com.au

Sydney

- ► Sydney Morning Herald (SMH) www.smh.com.au
- ► The Daily Telegraph www.dailytelegraph.com.au
- ► The Sun-Herald www.heraldsun.com.au
- ► The Sunday Telegraph www.dailytelegraph.com.au

The existence of the internet and the proliferation of social media enable most Brits to keep an active interest in UK news and global celebrity gossip.

Sport, in particular, is always a topic of debate – especially when the age-old cricket, tennis, or rugby trophies are at stake.

ONLINE

In addition to traditional media extensions that have websites online, Australia has a rich internet community and high adoption of internet use. There has been a recent trend towards digital-only media offerings in place of traditional magazines. Large, independent online communities exist, along with communities built from niches such as small business owners, expats, parents, and women.

Social media, especially, has a high take-up in Australia, with some of the highest usage of Twitter and Facebook in the world.

Some popular websites for current affairs and lifestyle:

www.abc.net.au/news
www.mamamia.com.au
www.yahoo7.com.au
www.womensagenda.com.au
www.anthillonline.com/category/topic
www.getfrank.com.au

RADIO

The majority of radio stations, with the exception of ABC and SBS, are, unsurprisingly, regional. Many of the commercial brands such as Triple J or Nova are national, with a local broadcast covering traffic, news, and weather.

Sensationalist DJs seem to have made the press globally of late. There is general male DJ culture of outspokenness, pranks, and a 'lad'/'larrikin' vibe. The music scene is quite behind here, so don't expect to know about the latest and greatest via the media here. Should you wish to keep abreast of the latest in the music industry, or what's happening in the UK, it's best to look to the UK media to stay up-to-date.

TELEVISION

Free to View

Free-to-view television in Australia is just that – it does not require a TV licence, as in the UK. Just plug in and view.

There are five main broadcasters at time of writing. Each has a primary channel (e.g. ITV in the UK) as well as off-shoot channels with an extended offering of general entertainment, often repeats.

Channel 7, 7Two, 7mate
Channel 9 (or WIN), GEM, Go!
Channel 10, Eleven, One
SBS One, SBS Two, SBS HD
ABC1, ABC2

All TV channels have a decent online presence offering catch-up TV and bonus extras.

Whilst there is a growing TV production scene in Australia, a large proportion of imported programming comes from both the US and UK.

Channels 7, 9, and 10 are typical commercial stations – similar to ITV.

ABC is a publicly funded station with a charter to meet certain programming obligations. It has a focus on current affairs, documentaries, and light entertainment. Many imported BBC UK programs can be viewed here.

SBS is a 'hybrid-funded' public station catering to a multi-lingual and multi-cultural audience. Much of the programming is drama, food, or documentary-related, with foreign language news and current affairs. UK imports are popular here too – often quirky Channel 4 offerings.

Again, with the proliferation of the internet and iTunes, we don't suffer from being Down Under. Some of the programming is quickly broadcast after the US, or at least available for downloading.

PAY TV – SATELLITE

Pay TV is provided by Foxtel. As with Sky in the UK, multiple packages are on offer with varying contract terms and pricing. The familiar lifestyle, sports, and movie channels abound here. Many UK and US imports are available for viewing, with the usual volume of repeats. Visit www.foxtel.com.au for more information.

POSTAL SERVICES AND ADDRESSES

Postal deliveries are daily in urban regions, Monday–Friday (public holidays excepted).

Stamps can be bought at any post office or at various retail outlets, such as newsagents and convenience stores. You can find postage pricing, tracking, and other information on the Australia Post website: auspost.com.au.

The postal system is fairly efficient here. Within each state and main metro region, post is typically delivered within a couple of days. Distance, of course, plays a part, so a postal item that needs to cross the country from Sydney to Perth, for example, will likely take three to five days. Overseas postage is relatively fast during normal periods, considering the distance. A letter back to the UK will take about a week, give or take a couple of days (though expect this to take longer at busy times such as Christmas and Easter).

Australian street addresses comprise of a unit (apartment) number, street number, suburb, state, and postcode. Even though a suburb or area is in Sydney or Melbourne, the city name in terms of its address is only mentioned if it is the main central business district (CBD) area. The suburb is then followed by the state, abbreviated as below.

For example, Bondi is a suburb within Sydney, but an address would be written like so for a house (or unit):

Joe Blogs
1 The Street (or 1/1 The Street)
Bondi
NSW 2026

Postcodes for all main capital cities are four digits and end in 000. Suburbs have an incremental number based on the distance from the CBD (2009 is closer to the CBD than 2048, for example):

Adelaide, SA 5000

Brisbane, QLD 4000

Melbourne, VIC 3000

Perth, WA 6000

Sydney, NSW 2000

PUBLIC HOLIDAYS

The number of public holidays varies by state, and dates for common holidays such as the Queen's Birthday and Labour Day also differ by state. If a public holiday lands on a weekend, the following Monday will typically be declared a holiday. Public holidays that happen to land on a weekday are taken on that day. This is unlike the UK, where public holidays are generally moved to the Friday or Monday to create a long weekend.

Common to all states are:

New Year's Day

Australia Day – 26 January

Good Friday

Easter Monday

Anzac Day – 25 April

Queen's Birthday

Labour Day

Christmas Day

Boxing Day

For up-to-date information, visit http://australia.gov.au/topics/australian-facts-and-figures/public-holidays.

Bank Holidays are different to public holidays and, again, vary by state. Only banks and financial institutions are closed on these days.

RULES AND REGULATIONS

Overall, Australia is a fairly relaxed nation. However, there are some useful rules and regulations that it pays to know about.

DRINKING AND SMOKING

The legal drinking age is 18-years-old. The purchase of alcohol takes place separately from other items, so it is very uncommon to see alcohol being sold in supermarkets, for example. There is usually a liquor store nearby for convenience. This is slowly changing, with international stores such as Costco and Aldi selling alcohol on the same premises. However, the licence requires payment for alcohol products to be separate on designated tills.

Smoking laws vary by state. In general, Australia has a very low tolerance for smoking. This was further reinforced in 2012 by federal government plain packaging legislation. No branding is permitted on tobacco packaging, and no advertising or display of tobacco products is allowed anywhere that sells them. You will simply find a product price list. Buying tobacco involves knowing what you want rather than being able to peruse a selection.

In general, it is illegal to smoke in enclosed spaces and within a few metres of access points to enclosed spaces. Outdoor spaces in restaurants and bars are subject to laws concerning how big the outdoor space is as a proportion of the entire area. Some establishments will enforce a total smoking ban for the comfort of all guests.

DROUGHT, FIRE, AND WATER RESTRICTIONS

Australia's climate and drought-prone landscape is sadly an all too common challenge with often fatal consequences. Bush fires are a huge challenge, resulting in a healthy respect for fire and water. In the summer months, especially, fire risk is widely publicised in areas close to bushland and prone to fire.

It is very common to have area-wide fire bans and other restrictions to help minimise fire risk. The Bureau of Meteorology (www.bom.gov.au) also publicises any water restrictions that may be in force. Water is a scarce resource in Australia, with recycling and desalination making very slow progress in the minds of Aussies who are used to consuming pure water.

EQUALITY, FREEDOM, AND CULTURE

Australia is a socially tolerant nation. Everyone is equal in the eyes of the law, regardless of age, colour, sex, beliefs, or religion, with a general freedom of speech and association. This is partly how the expression 'fair go' was coined – regardless of your background or history, everyone has the opportunity to achieve.

One aspect of Australian culture which shocks some Brits is the 'macho' and blunt undertone. There is an overall laidback nature to communications. Honesty is expected and reciprocated; this can sometimes come across as rudeness. Formalities don't play a large role in society here, and the casual approach to personal interaction can surprise many newcomers. Sports, teasing/joking, and, mateship, can add up to an overt 'blokey-ness' which can be intimidating to new arrivals. It is often said that someone making fun of someone ('taking the piss') is a signal of esteem. Whilst there is usually no harm intended, the Australian sense of humour can sometimes be perceived as chauvinistic, so it pays to keep an open mind during the adjustment period.

GENERAL ETIQUETTE

Generally, personal space is respected, and it is not common to be overtly touchy-feely or within arm's length when in conversation.

Etiquette in the form of social niceties exists, albeit delivered in a casual way – 'please', 'thank you', and 'excuse me' are all appreciated and the norm. First names, often abbreviated, in nickname form, or a variation of the surname are common, with a minimum of formality. I can hardly remember the last time I was called Sharon by anyone other than new acquaintances – with most preferring to call me Shaz, Shazza, or Swifty!

Tipping in restaurants is generally not required, although, given people travel more and are exposed to differing cultures, tips for good service are becoming the new norm. Note that service charges and credit card fees may be in addition to what you have ordered. Some restaurants may impose a public holiday surcharge to their bill and should publicise this on menus or upon entering. When settling your bill in a casual establishment, even if there is table waiter service, it is quite normal to walk to the till or cashier to make payment rather than do so at your table. In formal establishments, the usual asking for the bill and making payment at your table is the norm.

If invited to a BBQ or someone's home, it is customary to bring a bottle of wine or six pack of beer. It also pays to ask if you can bring your own meat or a side dish as a contribution to the proceedings.

WALKING AND CYCLING

Jay walking is illegal in Australia. Each road crossing has a pedestrian stop and go light, and crossing when red is not permitted. When queuing/waiting on an escalator or walking up and down stairs, it is generally accepted that you do so on the left-hand side.

Cyclists must wear a helmet when riding their bicycles – this law is becoming more necessary given the increased uptake in cycling within urban areas. Lights and fluorescent clothing are advisable and are a legal requirement in the dark or conditions with reduced visibility. Laws on this matter are state imposed, so it is best to check within your home state.

STAYING IN TOUCH – TIME DIFFERENCES

There is no denying that the matter of time difference is confusing for some. Most family and friends you leave behind will struggle with this concept. It's guaranteed that you will be woken in the middle of the night by someone who has forgotten you are on the opposite side of the planet!

Australia spans different time zones, as below. Note that 'UTC' means Universal Coordinated Time, the standard that has replaced GMT and helps avoid confusion about daylight savings times:

▶ ACDT Australian Central Daylight Time UTC + 10.5 hours
  (Adelaide in summer)

▶ ACST Australian Central Standard Time UTC + 9.5 hours
  (Adelaide in winter)

- ▶ AEDT Australian Eastern Daylight Time UTC + 11 hours
  (Sydney and Melbourne in summer)

- ▶ AEST Australian Eastern Standard Time UTC + 10 hours
  (Sydney and Melbourne in winter; Brisbane all year)

- ▶ AWDT Australian Western Daylight Time UTC + 9 hours
  (Perth in summer)

- ▶ AWST Australian Western Standard Time UTC + 8 hours
  (Perth in winter)

As in the UK, daylight savings is in operation from spring (first Sunday in October at 2am), reverting to standard time in autumn (first Sunday in April at 2am). "Spring forward, Fall back."

These tools are invaluable when working out the time in different cities – handy for those family and friend phonecalls to determine 'when it's 9am there, what time is it here?': www.timeanddate.com/worldclock/meeting.html or www.worldtimebuddy.com.

UNITS OF MEASUREMENT

Australia uses the metric system. Length is in centimetres, metres, or kilometres; weight in grams or kilograms; the Australian Dollar is worth 100 cents. Weather is conveyed in °C. This takes some getting used to – especially in terms of distance, body height, and weight when we're used to thinking in pounds, miles, feet, and inches.

Using a tool such as www.metric-conversions.org is helpful to familiarise yourself with your own 'stats', such as your height and weight.

1 mile = 1.6 kilometres
1 foot = 30.48 centimetres
1 lb = 0.45 kilograms
1 stone = 6.35 kilograms
1 kilogram = 2.2 lbs
1 kilometre = 0.62 miles
1 metre = 3.28 feet

It's common for most people to spend the first months, even years, furiously converting back to feet, £ Sterling, and miles to find a fair point of comparison. This is perfectly normal, but it will help you to feel more integrated if you learn a few basics, like your own height and weight using the metric system, to help speed up this process. Making conversions back to £ Sterling is initially useful, although you will likely have a different salary here, and it pays to think about costs in relation to your current earnings and disposable income to ensure you have a fair comparison.

WATER

Tap water in Australia is safe to drink. It is a legal requirement that if water is not safe to drink (i.e. tank or bore water) that this is clearly marked.

Tap/drinking water is not recycled in Australia. There is a great 'yuck' factor that exists, but there are motions towards desalination or recycling to offer more sustainable solutions. Instead, water here is 'harvested' in catchments, reservoirs, or dams.

We suffer occasional periods of nervousness when droughts occur, dam levels are low, and water restrictions are put in force. This is a fact of life here and, of course, varies according to where you are in the country and its climatic conditions. Extremes of bushfires, floods, and drought have been reported in the global media over recent years, attributed to global climate change – also widely publicised. The best course of action is to keep up-to-date with local news, alongside a dose of common sense – to determine an appropriate level of caution.

Chapter re-cap –
I don't understand...

+ You're in and set-up. The honeymoon and excitement of everything being new might start to wear off.

+ You just want to understand how things work and go about your business.

+ Simple tasks may seem hard, and you will feel like you stand out as people notice you're a newbie.

+ No one told you how hard it can be and a host of other things you'll quickly learn in this phase.

+ Disappointment and loneliness might set in. It's time to stay strong, positive, and focused. Take the time and effort to take everything in, be observant, and understand the culture.

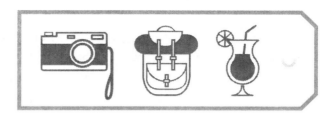

STEP 6

EXPLORE AND DISCOVER

An important part of settling in and feeling at home is understanding the culture of your new home. This will take time to learn and discover, and it will possibly involve some 'unlearning' in the meantime. Adapting to your new environment is key, rather than expecting it to be like home and trying to change people or behaviours.

I made this mistake when I arrived here and put myself months, possibly even years, behind in the process of feeling at home. I wasn't interested in sport so didn't engage in any Monday morning conversations about the weekend's matches. I didn't understand why it was necessary to shorten every single word, continuing to say presentation instead of presso, afternoon rather than arvo. I struggled to understand the lingo and didn't make an effort to learn it. The fact is, I had read and heard a lot about the Aussie lifestyle without appreciating how different it actually can be. This wasn't helped by the fact that many of the people I met were fellow Brits, so my not changing didn't really matter to them. Slowly, as does happen, one by one, they returned to the UK or moved on. It was almost as though I had to start again when almost all of my friends left and I had little social circle to speak of. Life couldn't be better for me now – I've expanded my social circle in different ways and feel truly ensconced in the lifestyle here – but it was not without a struggle and a feeling of isolation, mostly brought on by my unconscious stubbornness to adapt and be more open to opportunities.

Many UK expats arrive thinking they know what to expect or, worse still, believe that the Aussie way of life is exactly the same as in the UK, just with a different accent and more sun! The latter is certainly not the case, and, based on feedback from many an expat here, it's difficult to accurately predict what to expect.

Aussies are sports mad, competitive, open, informal, and patriotic. In general, they work to live, and family is very important. Regardless of whether an Aussie avidly follows sport, they will know what games are happening and will always know the result. It's part of Australian DNA to have an interest in sporting events, if only to ensure that a conversation can be sparked about the result. Proud of the lifestyle that this country offers, most Aussies love the outdoors and anticipate the summer, which, by default, means barbies, Christmas, beach time, and socialising. Aussies don't take themselves too seriously, and honesty and being forthright in communicating is to be expected, which comes as a shock to many.

Gambling and drinking are both accepted and the norm here, although they occasionally pop up as the centre of social debate. Healthy living and care of the environment is encouraged, with an active lifestyle achievable for most due to the fair weather and facilities available.

Children

Australia is a great place for children growing up, and Australians place a strong importance on family life. Parents and children are served well in terms of activities, and children are welcome most anywhere. The great outdoors, beach culture, and Australia's rich array of wildlife are just the start of the fun.

Being outdoors is the most popular option and a very cheap way to entertain children. Most urban areas of the capital cities have parks with play areas – and, of course, there's normally a beach nearby. Given the beach and water lifestyle, a large majority of children in Australia are comfortable in the water, swim regularly, and participate in Nippers, where large groups of children and their parents converge at beaches on summer weekend mornings, and the children learn about water safety, surf conditions, rocks, and marine life. Nippers is considered important for children aged 5–13. For more information, visit sls.com.au/nippers.

School sports activities and children's get togethers quite often rule the family weekend. Australians are a sociable bunch and don't need much excuse for a picnic or barbie. This keeps everyone busy during term-time weekends, with school camps and activities a popular option to keep children occupied during the school holidays.

All of the capital cities have museums, wildlife parks and zoos for a more educational experience. For more information, you can refer to the 'out and about' section a little later in this chapter.

WEB RESOURCES FOR PARENTS

The internet and online forums and communities are popular here, not least for parents looking for inspiration and advice on a range of topics.

Here are a few popular sites to get you started:

www.essentialbaby.com.au
www.webchild.com.au
www.kidspot.com.au
www.bubhub.com.au
raisingchildren.net.au
parentingaustralia.com.au
www.swimkids.com.au

Eating and drinking

ALCOHOL AND BYO

At the time of writing, with the recent exception of Aldi and Costco, all alcohol is sold through liquor or bottle shops.

You may prefer to source wine or your favourite beer from a local bottle shop. Otherwise, you can look to the national chains. Coles will sometimes have a Liquorland or First Choice Liquor alongside or nearby their supermarkets. Likewise, Woolworths is owned by the same group as BWS, which is standalone but often found with a Woolworths nearby. Quite common here are drive through bottle shops – very convenient.

Dan Murphy's is by far the largest nationwide chain and offers a huge range of everything alcoholic at competitive prices.

A vast range of beautiful Australian wines can be found in bottle shops. Wineries' cellar doors are also a good way to explore wines, and most will ship nationwide.

The concept of BYO alcohol is popular in Australia. Although, with licensing laws becoming more relaxed and costs to be a licenced establishment having decreased over the years, this is not as common as in times gone by. Still, many restaurants will allow you bring your own beer or wine (note that many will only allow wine) and will charge a corkage fee. This will vary by restaurant and will be charged by the number of people drinking per bottle, but it can be a great way to take the sting out of the cost of dining out.

CAFÉ CULTURE

Pretty much everywhere in Australia can be said to have a café culture. The ritual of collecting a morning coffee in a paper cup on the way to work will be experienced all over the country. Aussies place a lot of importance on this ceremony and are known to follow their barista rather than a particular café to ensure consistency in their morning caffeine fix. If you are a coffee lover, you too will become familiar with this habit. If you don't drink coffee, there is tea and a multitude of other refreshments; but, ultimately, you will still 'meet for a coffee' no matter your poison.

EATING OUT

Breakfast, brunch, lunch, dinner, tapas, canapés – Aussies also love to eat out. Heading out for brekky or brunch over the weekend with friends, or simply for your own sustenance, is customary for most Aussies. Even if only once in a while, eating out for the first meal of the day is an activity you will become familiar with.

Grabbing lunch is also somewhat of a ritual any day of the week. The food court concept is common and popular here, where you can peruse a choice of vendors in one place and have food cooked to order or choose from a prepared selection. Even sandwiches can be freshly made to order in cafes or delis, and it's rare to find packaged sandwiches to grab and go. It's more common to find an Asian noodle bar with a variety of readymade hot food to choose from or pasta bars which will pack and go! This is ever so slightly changing as the well-travelled amongst us start to demand what we see overseas, and the pace of life forces us to consider faster meal options.

A fantastic testament to the rich diversity of cultures that exists here is the selection and variety of cuisines available. In most cities, you will find anything ranging from Afghan to Peruvian, from Vietnamese to Indian, sushi to churrasco, top-notch French to Tex-Mex. You will find your favourite foods or something new to try here. Australia is passionate to the point of obsessed with the quality of its food and availability of produce, and this attracts the most esteemed of international chefs and restaurants.

Australian cuisine covers a broad spectrum. Bush tucker or indigenous food is hunt-and-gather fare. Kangaroo and a wide range of native plants are considered nutritious, tasty, and unique, although not available on a wide scale. Some 'mod Oz', that is, modern Australian, restaurants do like to showcase food of the land. More commonly, mod Oz cuisine can be described as 'Western' fare with a fusion of diverse influences. It combines a range of techniques and flavours from around the world. Fresh produce and seasonality, much like any fine cuisine, are a key component; after that, pretty much anything goes.

No mention of Australian fare would be complete without the mention of the BBQ or 'barbie'. Aussies will literally put anything on the barbie – snags (sausages), prawns (not shrimp as the saying goes!), steaks, 'roo (kangaroo), vegetables, even fruit and desserts. The more traditional roasts and slow-cooked stews pay homage to Aussies' English heritage, along with a 'cuppa'. Typical Aussie takeaway food ranges from fish and chips to meat pies, with curries, noodles, and sushi rolls all an integral part of the takeaway spectrum.

Eating out with food allergies or intolerances or particular preferences is very achievable, and most cafés and restaurants commonly cater for vegetarians, vegans, and nut allergies. Specials requests are also accepted as a way of life over here and will usually be accommodated with minimal fuss.

Each winter, the Australian Good Food Guide issues reviews of restaurants all over the country, awarding any notable efforts with a 'Chef's Hat'. This is the closest Australia has to the Michelin Star awards and a good way of identifying outstanding restaurants: www.agfg.com.au.

For more ideas about finding great food in Australia, take a look at these websites:

- ▶ Eatability is a comprehensive website, a Tripadvisor of sorts, where you can read diner reviews of restaurants: www.eatability.com.au.

- ▶ Fairfax's Good Food guide is a useful reference for foodies wanting a fix of local food news and happenings: www.goodfood.com.au.

- ▶ Another restaurant review site: www.bestrestaurants.com.au.

- ▶ The Entertainment Book is a great reference and resource when you're first starting out, with each edition covering a different geographic range. It offers discounts amongst a large range of restaurants, services, and activities. You can often get 25% off meals at top restaurants: www.entertainmentbook.com.au.

DRINKING OUT

Australia, regardless of where you are, is not short of watering holes – called bars, hotels, and pubs. The terminology was a little confusing for me to begin with. Traditional pubs are generally called 'hotels' given their tendency in the past to offer accommodation. Confusingly, many do not offer accommodation these days! Most will offer traditional style food which is generally more rustic. Bars tend be more upmarket, offering a higher level of service and ambience, with a wider choice of beverages on offer. The food here will tend to be more sophisticated, if offered.

FOOD SHOPPING

Food shopping in Australia can be as exciting or as simple as you make it. This very much depends on your culinary skills and how adventurous you are with your cooking at home.

Supermarkets are, of course, an obvious place to start. National chains Coles, Woolworths, and IGA have a solid footprint across the country. For all intents and purposes, these are the equivalent to Tesco and Sainsbury's. IGA is unique in that it is franchised and sells products very specific to the local market. It is quite usual to go to an IGA in a Chinatown to find almost their entire range is Asian. Down the road at an IGA in the Italian quarter, you can close your eyes and be fooled into thinking you're in Italy, with specific Italian cuts of meat, a large Italian deli, and largely Italian everything else. There is also a handful of supermarkets that exist in individual states only, such as Supabarn in ACT and NSW only.

Aussie supermarkets have been typically very unexciting places to shop in the past with dreary shops and uninspiring quality. This has mostly been due to a lack of competition and Australia's very small population. In comparison to the likes of the densely populated UK, it is a very small market distributed over a large land mass. The weekly shop was never so boring as when I first arrived in 2005. Retail in general struggled to put the consumer first, prices were relatively high, and the experience dull.

The tide, however, has changed over the past few years, as with many things here in Australia. The consumer is benefitting hugely. Overseas retailers such as Costco and Aldi are aggressively expanding, resulting in hotter competition. In addition, the likes of Coles have imported management and retail executives from the UK, which has breathed new life into the landscape. Opening hours have followed suit, and most supermarkets are open early in the morning until late into the evening, with many in central and urban areas open until midnight or 24 hours. Note that shopping-centre opening hours may exceed those of the retailers within it.

After being here a few weeks, I realised that, whilst the 'weekly shop' does exist here, to get the selection and quality of food we were used to, we would end up shopping the old-fashioned way. That is, visiting a butcher for meat, a grocer or market for fruit and vegetables, the fishmonger for fish, and so on. Buying alcohol here mostly involves a separate transaction, so, all in all, it can be more time-consuming depending on your tastes and preferences.

There are other subtle nuances you will find here, such as differences in terminology. A rib-eye steak is called a scotch fillet, sirloin is New York and so on – it takes getting used to, but you will find some butchers will be able to help 'translate' for you. You'll appreciate the distance much more when you realise that French cheeses are very expensive (although the local range of dairy is very good), and you can't nip to Marks & Spencers for an expansive range of ready meals to make life easier. (Although, hot off the press at time of writing are rumours that Marks & Spencers will be coming to Australia).

Ready meals and gourmet foreign cheeses are two examples of foods that firmly fit into the speciality arena, and you will need to seek out a deli or provedore with a fromagerie for your cheese plate or a gourmet grocer to have something prepared to heat up at home. The trend of ready meals doesn't exist on the same scale here as in the UK, although this is slightly changing. Eating out tends to be more common, and the culture of heating up food is not really that popular here. Urban regions are well served with food delivery options.

Another thing you will notice is a great range of produce that you may or may not recognise, or that features more prominently here than in the UK. Shopping here tends to be seasonal, as imported goods tend to be much more expensive. You'll notice more exotic fruits like pineapples and mangoes are common and relatively cheap when in season and will either be very expensive or not available at all when not in season. This is different to my experience in the UK, where it is common to find the same produce range available year around, with the culture of importing much more accepted.

A preference for alternative ingredients, or the need to shop for intolerances or allergies, will be easy to satisfy. You don't have to search too hard in a supermarket to find gluten, dairy, or nut-free alternatives and you will be even better served in a good range of health food shops. Organic farming and produce is becoming more popular, although the price difference has meant a relatively slow uptake.

If you're craving foods from home, a couple of websites such as www.britishsweets.com.au and www.treatsfromhome.com.au will deliver your British favourites, from Bisto to Hula Hoops! Some branches of Coles and Woolworths, mostly in urban areas, also offer sections catering for a range of expat cravings. My local Coles and Woolies have ranges catering for Irish, South African, Dutch, and British expats selling Alpen, Irn Bru, and Paxo. You may occasionally have a pang for English chocolate, biscuits, and crisps – they just don't taste the same here. Having said that, you'll find a large range of other foods that will offer novelty factor, so don't panic. Don't despair about Marmite, tea, HP sauce, or Heinz baked beans – all are easily available here. Items like baked beans actually have an 'English Recipe' variety which is made under licence here and comes quite close to the original.

Entertainment, culture, and the arts

The arts scene in Australia is thriving, although arguably not as mature as that in the UK, and, indeed, nearby Europe. Added to the mix is the indigenous influence on both visual and performing arts, which is unique and well worth exploring. Good places to start are Ticketek or Ticketmaster. These are ticketing portals that offer tickets for almost anything from music concerts to the ballet and art galleries. Their websites offer the chance to explore the venues in each city, and from here you can register to receive news from the venues themselves or select the updates from the central sites. Most events will also be advertised in the newspapers and on their respective websites.

Many artists, performance and otherwise, enjoy touring in Australia. It is common to have a regular calendar of British and American performers conduct national tours of Australia. From Cirque du Soleil to comedians, Elton John to Beyoncé, it can be fairly straightforward to get tickets to events due to the smaller population and range of venues.

Festivals of all kinds – arts, cultural, fashion, food, wine, writers, music – are popular in Australia. The best course of action is to keep up to date with your city's events; there will likely be a selection for you to enjoy every year.

Cinema is a popular form of entertainment. It can be expensive, but there is always a 'cheap' day where tickets are $10. The cheap day happens to be Tuesday in Sydney, and it varies by state and city rather than individual cinemas.

A good place to start for all movie news and times is yourmovies. com.au, where you can select any location, day or movie. There are 3 national cinema chains:

www.eventcinemas.com.au
www.palacecinemas.com.au
www.hoyts.com.au

Others, like www.dendy.com.au and www.villagecinemas.com.au, are limited to certain states. There are a number of independent and arts cinemas in each city and an IMAX 3D cinema based in Sydney and Melbourne.

Many cities also have an open air cinema in the summer time. Check out www.moonlight.com.au. Best to google 'open air cinema' in your city to get up-to-date listings.

Exploring your city and getting away

Most expats in Australia tend to enjoy travelling and will choose to take advantage of their time here to travel across the country as well as making the most of their local area. The disadvantage to living in such a huge country is that you can spend a lot of time travelling without experiencing much new – unlike in Europe, where you can fly an hour in different directions and be firmly amongst another culture, immersed in a different environment and language. However, there is so much of interest to discover, the distance ends up being a quirk of the whole experience.

Getting out and about is an important part of integrating and discovering your new environment. Day and weekend trips help you to realise that you're somewhere completely different. Once work and the routine starts to get settle down, it's a good idea to escape the rat race every once in a while. Another great benefit to living in Oz is, of course, having the gorgeous beaches and great weather – there's no doubt that you'll have ample opportunity to experience this, wherever you have decided to settle.

BEACHES, SWIMMING, AND THE SUN

Much of the Australian lifestyle is characterised by images of the beach and water. All five main capitals are situated close to the coastline – some slightly farther than others, but all within 30–60 minutes' drive away. Sydney is famous for its beaches, of which there are about 45 around Sydney Harbour and the ocean. Other cities are in close proximity but not directly situated so closely to the water.

Most frequented surf beaches will have lifeguards or at least flags indicating the area in which it's safe to swim or that the area is being guarded. Many ocean beaches will also have saltwater or beach pools which are more protected than the ocean and surf. Some harbour or quieter beaches will have shark nets for those areas where sharks (or nursing sharks) may be more likely.

Nowhere in Australia is immune from shark attacks. Surfers, distance swimmers, or daredevils will be more at risk, of course, as they are active farther from the coast. Proceed with caution, stay within the flags, and remain alert is the best advice.

Last, but certainly not least – the sun. It is common knowledge that there isn't much of an ozone layer above Australia. This has fatal consequences. Australia has the highest incidence of skin cancer in the world. Approximately two in three Australians will be diagnosed with cancer before the age of 70 (according to www.skincancer.gov.au).

Whilst there is an outdoor culture, there is also a healthy respect for the sun. Sunscreen is widely available in very large bottles – and not many stores will carry sunscreen with less than an SPF of 30. You will burn if unprotected, so heed caution and ensure that you are armed with waterproof sunscreen and that all moisturisers and cosmetics contain SPF. Hats are commonly part of school uniforms, and sunscreen sometimes available at outdoor events.

DAY TRIPS: TOP THREE BY CITY

ADELAIDE

Adelaide is a small and compact city, and a short drive can land you in a different world.

1. Hahndorf and Adelaide Hills are an easy half-hour drive from Adelaide. Hahndorf itself is an old German settlement and, today, a popular tourist attraction featuring craft shops and a quaint village ambience. Adelaide Hills is a cool climate region, where berries, grapes, and other ingredients are grown and sold. Pick-your-own farms and cellar doors will welcome you.

2. The wine regions of the Barossa Valley, Clare Valley, and McLaren Vale must feature on your to-do list if you live in, or are visiting,

Adelaide. All have formidable reputations for fabulous wines – the Barossa and McLaren Vale for bold and juicy reds and the Clare most known for its Rieslings and unique Shiraz.

3. Kangaroo Island is a unique sanctuary located a 45 minute ferry ride away from Cape Jervis, south of Adelaide, or a short flight from the city's airport. It is a pristine animal haven, with a large part of the island declared a conservation area and national park. Unique flora and fauna can be seen here, and it is also popular with food and wine enthusiasts, with fresh seafood and produce grown here.

BRISBANE

Brisbane is the only city not based on a beach, so it's no coincidence that most day trips involve a short drive towards the ocean and a great variety of options by the sea.

1. The Gold Coast makes a great day out, especially if you have children, at roughly one hour's drive from Brisbane. There are huge, long beaches, theme parks, and hinterland bush walks – something for everyone. Water is definitely a theme of most parks here – with Seaworld, Wet 'n' Wild, and White Water World all very popular, especially during school holidays.

2. Just under two hours north of Brisbane is Noosa Heads (shortened to 'Noosa') on the Sunshine Coast. A great playground for shopping, spa treats, and great eateries, Noosa is set on a lush hinterland, with expansive beaches and a relaxed, laid-back feel. Great for a city escape or weekend getaway.

3. Byron Bay is a stunning spot two hours south of Brisbane. In the far north of NSW, on the coast, Byron is a great place to see the

sun rise at the lighthouse, surf, whale watch, shop, or eat – or all of the above. It's a popular weekend getaway spot and is known for its alternative lifestyle vibe and as a haven for meditation and yoga retreats, blues music festivals, and arts and crafts.

MELBOURNE

There is plenty to occupy the most discerning of travellers, in Melbourne – from a day out in St Kilda or Brighton, to exploring the city's laneways, or, of course, shopping. If you're itching to get out and about, there are some great options.

1. Favourites on any tourist checklist are the Dandenong Ranges and the Yarra Valley. An hour or so to the northwest of Melbourne, you can explore the quaint villages and forests of the Dandenong region and carry on to the Yarra for some wine tasting and plenty of places to enjoy a snack or meal. A little farther along and you can take in some wildlife at the Healesville Sanctuary.

2. Oceans – The Great Ocean Road is an iconic route, taking in the Twelve Apostles along the western coastline south west of Melbourne, around Port Phillip and past Geelong. The towns of Torquay, Lorne, and Apollo Bay through to Warnambool provide great pit stops and scenery along the way. From the east of Melbourne, and all the way around the other side of Port Phillip, you will reach the pretty spot of Sorrento at the tip of Port Phillip Bay on the east. Another wine region on the Mornington Peninsula offers some more typically Victorian wines, taking on a different character due to the marine cooler climate.

3. Spa Country – 1.5 hours to the north and slightly west of Melbourne is the pretty Daylesford and Macedon Ranges area with mineral water springs, pretty lakes, and spa treats.

PERTH

Life in Perth is laid-back and family orientated. Your days will most likely be spent by the beach or pool. If you want to get out and about, a drive or ferry ride can get you away.

1. Fremantle is a short 20-minute drive south of Perth and is home to the city's port. With a large market, local arts and craft shops, an antique strip, and eateries, there is plenty to do for a day out here.

2. Rottnest Island – half an hour on a ferry from Fremantle and you will be immersed in the beauty that is Rottnest – over 60 beaches, a nature reserve with unique flora and fauna, golf and other activities; this is a perfect day out from Perth. It is one of the few places in the world where you can find a native quokka, otherwise known as a kangaroo rat, due to the lack of predators on the island.

3. Possibly more of a weekend trip than a day out, given the 2.5–3 hour drive, no stay in Perth is complete without a visit to the Margaret River region. This region is home to top boutique wine producers with wines said to rival the best French Bordeaux, beaches with great surf breaks, whale watching, microbreweries, and a thriving gourmet scene.

SYDNEY

Life in Sydney can be fairly hectic, but, within a few hours, you can be truly out of the hustle and bustle. The huge range of beaches up and down the coast and within the harbour can help shed the stress of the toughest of weeks. Otherwise, there are a number of excursion options for those wishing to escape the city:

1. Blue Mountains – 1–1.5 hours directly west of the city are these gorgeous mountains, so named because of the blue haze emitted by the gum trees. There are lovely walks (be sure to stay firmly on the tracks so as not to get lost), a funicular railway to a bush walk, a cable car, and some lovely towns like Leura and Blackheath for a lunch or coffee stop. If you want to explore a little farther, head to the Jenolan Caves and, on the way back, stop off at the Featherdale Wildlife Park for a truly Australian wildlife experience. You can extend this into a weekend trip and head to the boutique wine regions of either Orange or Mudgee for some beautiful scenery with great food and wine.

2. National Parks – one hour south of Sydney and along the coast, the Royal National Park is truly magnificent. Stunning views lie on the coast tracks, where you can easily not bump into another soul. An hour north of Sydney and Ku-ring-gai Chase National Park provides some breathtaking lookouts of the northern beaches area of Sydney (Whale Beach and Palm Beach), Pittwater, and the Hawkesbury River.

3. Hunter Valley – no stay in Australia is complete without a sample of the local wines, and the Hunter is one of the first Australian wine regions. The Hunter is two hours north of Sydney and offers pretty landscapes, the chance to sample great wines, and enjoyable lunches in a great range of local eateries.

OUT AND ABOUT – USEFUL RESOURCES

▶ Social Media – Facebook and Twitter are great ways to stay in touch; Australia is an early adopter of social media and is well connected.

▶ Weekend newspapers – these are a good way to get a feel for the events that run in your city. Most newspapers have sections with food reviews and the city's events that week.

▶ Time Out and Lonely Planet are great resources wherever you are in the world – you can buy the guidebook(s) for your city or visit their websites. With a sub-site on Time Out for each of the five main capital cities, this is a great reference if you're ever stuck for inspiration.

www.au.timeout.com
www.lonelyplanet.com
www.weekendnotes.com
www.scenemagazine.com.au (Brisbane)
www.experienceperth.com (Perth)
www.broadsheet.com.au (Sydney and Melbourne)
www.dailyaddict.com.au (Sydney and Melbourne)
www.theurbanlist.com (Sydney, Melbourne, Brisbane)

▶ Government websites and the 'city of...' sites are useful guides to overall Australia and your city's 'what's on' calendars:

Australia: www.australia.com
Adelaide: www.cityofadelaide.com.au/whats_on
Brisbane: www.brisbane.qld.gov.au/whats-on
Melbourne: www.thatsmelbourne.com.au
Perth: showmeperth.com.au
Sydney: whatson.cityofsydney.nsw.gov.au

▶ Event Tickets – the vast majority of event ticketing is managed by either Ticketek or Ticketmaster. These sites are a great place to start for sports, music, and theatre:

www.ticketek.com.au

www.ticketmaster.com.au

TRAVEL AND TRANSPORT

Domestic travel

Australia is a vast country spanning different terrains, landscapes, and coastlines. Whilst many Aussies travel frequently overseas, it's quite common to stay on home turf. After all, with the beaches, camping, bushwalking, snorkelling, diving, surfing, city breaks, national parks, and wilderness adventures, the range of leisure activities available is massive.

Many options involving the great outdoors can be cost effective and, in a lot of cases, free. Alas, unless you are camping, putting a roof over everyone's heads can be pricey – good accommodation doesn't come cheap in Australia, and eating out, cost of activities, and travel can bump up a family holiday's cost very quickly.

Air

There are only a few airlines serving the domestic market: Qantas, Jetstar (Qantas's no-frills airline), Virgin Australia, Rex, and Tiger Airways. All but Rex (flights to regional areas in Australia) have international offerings also. All are much of a muchness and compete on price. Virgin, Jetstar, and Tiger are all considered 'no-frills' and offer food and drink on board for an additional charge.

Flights, as always, will be priced according to supply and demand. Charges vary depending on popularity of the time of travel and number of flights/airlines serving that route. School holidays tend to be a high-traffic period, both domestically and internationally.

You can book flights through travel agents, via the airline websites direct, or through online portals such as www.expedia.com.au, www.lastminute.com.au, or www.webjet.com.au.

The longest flight time within Australia is around 5.5 hours for a flight from the East to West Coast – so, Brisbane or Sydney to Perth.

Driving

Driving is a less viable option for distant domestic travel, although many Aussies are not fazed by long stretches of driving. Melbourne to Sydney is a well traversed route, with the road links improving and widening each year. With a couple of short stops and light traffic, you can drive from centre to centre within about nine hours.

Train

Train travel in Australia can take considerable time and is definitely not always a cost-effective option, especially if you consider the time versus dollar ratio. There are, however, spectacular sceneries to be experienced. Famous train journeys such as The Ghan (North/South: Adelaide to Darwin via Alice Springs) and The Indian Pacific (East/West: Sydney to Perth via Adelaide) cover vast distances and allow travellers to enjoy the remoteness and sheer size of this beautiful country. These are potentially expensive trips, especially if you choose a cabin or berth option for extra comfort.

In general terms, the eastern and most populous side of the country is relatively well served for train travel between major cities and towns. Travel times are typically longer than if you were to drive, and will cost roughly the same as the lower end of the flight fare spectrum for the equivalent in air travel (if arriving at or departing from a major city). Town to town tends to be better served by train, although services are not fantastically frequent.

The different routes fall under the remit of various rail companies. You can find detailed maps, routes, and links to fare information here:

www.railmaps.com.au
www.railaustralia.com.au

Hotels and other accommodation

In relation to prices within the Australasia or Asia Pacific region, hotels in Australia tend to be quite expensive, though both ends of the price spectrum are well catered for, from camping and hostels through to high-end luxury hotels. Self-catering and holiday home rentals are also popular, especially for longer periods and larger groups or families.

Most of the international hotel groups are well represented in the main capital cities. Along with boutique hotels and smaller local chains, there are also serviced apartment options under national brands such as Quest and Oaks.

School, public, and summer holiday periods will inevitably be more expensive and will likely sell out far in advance.

In addition to the hotel websites direct and an internet search, you can try some of these popular sites:

www.wotif.com
www.lastminute.com.au
www.expedia.com.au
www.hotelscombined.com.au
www.stayz.com.au – listings for self-catering and holiday property rentals. Bookings tend to be direct with the property owners or their agents.
www.airbnb.com

International travel

The Australian Dollar has enjoyed increased buying power over the past few years, although at the time of writing it is dropping and this has significantly increased the appetite for international travel. It can be cheaper to spend time in Asia or the Pacific Islands than to enjoy a similar calibre of holiday in Australia – without having to necessarily spend much longer on the plane.

South East Asia and the Pacific Islands such as Fiji are common holiday destinations. Venturing farther afield to the US and Europe has also been popular, thanks to the strength of the currency and lower airfares. Fiji can be reached via a four-hour flight, and you can be sunning yourself in South East Asia after a seven-hour journey.

Australia is very well served for international travel. There are an unbelievable number of daily flights departing Australia, bound for Europe via Asia or the Middle East. The last I counted, when UK bound from Sydney, was 32 in one day. From Sydney alone – unbelievable! To think that many of these are A380 or jumbo aircraft carrying up to 400 passengers each – that's a lot of traffic, and most airlines enjoy full loads. Sydney and Melbourne are higher traffic cities for international travel. Options are available from Brisbane, Adelaide, and Perth, although they are less often and, therefore, may involve a domestic transit in addition to an Asian/Middle Eastern stop.

Whilst the market is competitive, the sheer distances involved result in higher fares than you'd be used to when hopping about within Europe. Fares are extremely variable; by way of loose example only – the lowest economy fares from Sydney or Melbourne to London I have seen available are around AU$1600 return. This can rise to the AU$2500–3000 mark for a busy period like Christmas, which will sell out far in advance. Many Brits take advantage of the long summer holiday by returning to the UK to visit family, and this also happens to be the high season for international visitors.

Travel agents are not as popular as online options but do still have a place in the market. You will recognise the likes of STA Travel and Flight Centre, both of which have a decent footprint in the big cities. Packages and tours are also popular and are heavily advertised in the weekend papers. Travellers are becoming savvier in terms of booking travel independently. The internet increasingly caters for this and will likely be your first port of call when investigating an overseas trip.

Shopping

Feeling familiar with where to source essential items is important to navigating a new life. In the early days, you will no doubt need to shop for a range of household items, clothes, and furniture.

In general, items will seem more expensive compared to the UK, even when the exchange rate is considered. This is the case even if you compare identical items like electronics, and it has been a bone of contention over the past few years. The rise in value of the dollar led many to believe that prices should, in fact, be going down, especially where imported items are concerned. At the same time, online shopping and the willingness of international retailers to deliver goods to Australia have led consumers to be more shopper savvy and have stumped many local retailers struggling to stay competitive in an economy where labour rates and property costs are relatively high.

Opening times in most urban areas and large shops are six or seven days per week, depending on the retailer. Smaller establishments will likely have shorter trading hours and may only be open for half the day on Saturday, if at all. This guide should help you to feel more certain about what to expect in your early days.

BANKS

Bank branches and their cash machines (called 'ATMs' here) are widely available in both urban and rural areas. Branch opening hours tend to vary depending on the local demand and tend to be 9.30am–4pm, but this will differ by day, branch, and other variables. Some city branches will offer longer opening hours, and Saturday opening is also starting to emerge.

Withdrawing cash from your own bank's ATM is free if you use their card or a card from their chosen network. However, withdrawal fees (determined by your bank) will kick in if you use an ATM belonging to another bank. There are also independently owned ATM machines in the likes of pubs, clubs, and other establishments. These will charge a fee regardless of your bank.

CREDIT CARD FEES

A supplementary fee to pay via your credit card is quite common in Australia. This is mostly due to credit card companies charging higher fees that many vendors choose to pass on rather than absorb. This is especially the case with American Express and Diners, for which you are sometimes charged a higher supplement, or which may not be accepted at all.

DEPARTMENT STORES

One-stop shopping is popular in Australia, with national department stores of varying quality meeting the demand.

David Jones is similar to John Lewis, will price match, and generally offers a good quality selection of almost anything you would need to buy, from cosmetics, appliances, electronics, and homewares, to clothing and shoes. Many David Jones stores have a food hall which is generally quite pricey, but it does offer an extensive range of quality and gourmet products that you may struggle to find elsewhere.

Myer is something like a cross between House of Fraser and Debenhams and the only real competitor to David Jones. Again, almost anything you will need is available here.

Big W, Target, and K-Mart are all discount department stores offering cheaper ranges of homeware, clothing, hardware, electronics, and so on. These can be best compared with a Wilko.

Peter's of Kensington is a Sydney-based institution of just one large shop. A rabbit warren of fantastic quality products at competitive prices, it offers a huge range of homeware, kitchenware, luggage and cosmetics. Fret not if you're out of Sydney; they ship Australia-wide via their website: www.petersofkensington.com.au.

A similar proposition to Peter's is Victoria's Basement. With a number of Sydney-based shops, the rest of Australia can enjoy their low prices and good range at www.victoriasbasement.com.au.

ELECTRONICS AND APPLIANCES

Harvey Norman and The Good Guys offer national coverage and online access to electronics and appliances. Make sure you ask for best pricing for even the smallest item; you will very likely get a discount. JB Hi-Fi is a good option for personal electronics, computers, and cameras.

Winnings Appliances is an institution, offering excellent family-owned service in NSW and QLD, along with a very large range of entry level to premium appliances in all of their stores. Camberwell Electrics is the nearest equivalent in VIC.

FASHION

Shopping for fashion in Australia can be expensive and of disappointing quality. The best reason I have heard for this is the need to create unique collections around our 'opposite' seasons, which vary from most of the western world. This is the case for the likes of imported high-street fashion brands like Zara and Jigsaw. The Australian fashion scene is unique partly for this reason and tends to be quite distinctive and quirky.

Top-end international designers sell their wares internationally and do not have market-specific collections. You will pay a premium to buy these brands here compared to in Europe.

Along with some of the usual suspects, like Jigsaw, Zara, and Topshop, there is a large range of high-street fashion you will find nationally: Witchery, Sportscraft, Country Road, Sheike, Sportsgirl, and David Lawrence, which compare to the likes of Hobbs, River Island,

and everything in between. Some of these offer men's clothing as well, in addition to Industrie, Oxford, and Marcs.

FURNITURE AND HOMEWARES

The usual suspect, Ikea, has at least one store in each of the five state capitals, with Melbourne and Sydney's populations large enough to warrant two.

King Furniture offers quality furniture across Australia, with Coco Republic offering a wider range of luxury furnishings in Melbourne, Sydney, and Queensland.

Domayne and Harvey Norman are all-in-one shops where you can buy everything from sofas to an outdoor setting.

Middle of the road and crowd pleaser Freedom offers a good range of almost everything you could need to set up your home, at a reasonable price.

At the bottom end of the spectrum, but a great option to set up quickly and cheaply, is Fantastic Furniture.

For beds, look to the department stores, Ikea, or Forty Winks and Snooze.

HABERDASHERY, CRAFTS, AND STATIONERY

If you need a needle and thread, some fabric, or enjoy crafts, you will find national chains Spotlight and Lincraft across Australia.

Officeworks is the best option for anything relating to office stationary, furniture, or electronics. They also have a handy printing facility in most stores.

HARDWARE

You will undoubtedly need to pick up some lightbulbs, plugs, or some gardening products at some stage. Bunnings offers the largest network of stores nationally, with others including Thrifty Link and Mitre 10. Bunnings is similar to a B&Q or Homebase.

IS THAT YOUR BEST PRICE?

Bargaining and asking for best deals is common and almost expected when buying certain big-ticket items and even smaller items like electronics. This is especially true if you are buying a number of items and can save you between 5–20% depending on what and how much you are buying, where you are shopping, and, in some cases, how you choose to pay. I know that, for many, this will seem strange and uncomfortable, but it can save valuable cash in your early days.

LAYBY

Layaway or layby may be offered at some retailers. This is essentially an agreement where the buyer pays instalments for an item that they don't want to (or cannot) pay for in one go. The seller stores the item until it is paid for in full. This is popular for those who may have bad credit and for whom repaying the debt through a credit card or other means is not possible.

LOYALTY PROGRAMS

The most popular loyalty programs in Australia tend to be frequent flyer and bank credit card programs where you accumulate points to redeem for flights or a selection of items available for purchase online.

Many stores will also have their own programs with varying degrees of generosity, and there is the flybuys program which is vaguely similar to the Nectar card in that it is accepted at a number of outlets such as Coles, K-Mart, and Coles petrol outlets. Woolworths has their 'Everyday Rewards' card which also links in to the Qantas Frequent Flyer program.

ONLINE

Online retail has quickly become very popular in Australia, and vendors are becoming savvy at offering their wares online. US and UK retailers, especially, have cashed in on the Aussie appetite to save money and get better value by making the most of the strong Australian dollar. This also opens the door to more choice as bricks and mortar shopping is quite behind in terms of the range of goods available compared to somewhere like the UK. Small and independent retailers wishing to have a wider reach and audience are also taking to the internet, to the benefit of us all. A quick search for almost anything you need will yield a plethora of vendors to meet your needs.

SECOND-HAND

Whether buying or selling second-hand goods, eBay is a good place to start. This is followed by Gumtree, popular as the ads are free. Aussies tend to enjoy shopping second-hand, especially for branded and designer goods. Charity shops, or 'op shops' as they are affectionately called here, are also popular for vintage finds and bargains. The same is true when you might be renovating or building; it is quite popular to consider second-hand for unique items or a cheaper alternative.

SHOPPING CENTRES AND HIGH STREETS, BY CITY

Shopping centre brand Westfield dominates the Australian shopping centre scene, and all major cities have a Westfield footprint. There is also a selection of other centres across the country, in addition to the classic 'high street' or CBD shopping area of each major city. Most shopping centres (but not those in CBDs) offer at least one hour of free parking, in many cases two or three hours. Many are also home to cinemas and eateries. Shopping centres are especially popular on steaming hot days, with many choosing to enjoy the air conditioning and a cool browse rather than bask in the sun on the beach!

Visit www.westfield.com.au to find your local shopping centre, their hours, and parking facilities.

The beauty of many Aussie cities is the vibrant suburb shopping available, in addition to the CBD and shopping centre offerings. Here is a start to finding your favourite street shopping area in your city:

ADELAIDE

Your retail fix in Adelaide can be satisfied along Rundle Mall in the CBD, Jetty Road in Glenelg, Unley Road in Unley, and Norwood Parade in Norwood.

BRISBANE

Shopping in Brisbane is improving and evolving: try Queen Street Mall, South Bank and Edward Street in the CBD, and James Street in Fortitude Valley, New Farm.

MELBOURNE

Shopping, especially for fashion, is fun in Melbourne. There is a wide choice and some great markets: visit Bourke Street Mall and surrounds in the CBD, Chapel Street in South Yarra, Queen Victoria Markets, South Melbourne Markets, Acland Street in St Kilda, Bay Street in Port Melbourne, Church Street in Brighton, and Bridge Road in Richmond.

PERTH

The compact city of Perth has a few shopping areas: Murray Street Mall, Hay Street Mall and Wesley Quarter in the CBD, the Market and High Street in Fremantle, Subiaco, and William Street in Northbridge.

SYDNEY

The 'city of villages', Sydney has a good selection of shopping areas in addition to the centres: Pitt Street Mall and surrounds in the CBD, Oxford Street in Paddington, Military Road in Mosman, The Corso in Manly, Norton Street and Marion Street in Leichhardt, Darling Street in Balmain, Surry Hills area, and King Street in Newtown.

THINK CAREFULLY BEFORE BUYING

This is a term you may see near a till, reminding you that the shop in question will not offer a refund if you decide that you simply don't want an item. In such a shop, a refund will only be offered it the item is found to be faulty – as part of your statutory rights. In most cases an exchange is possible, but many retailers are sticklers for having your receipt in any case as a proof of purchase. This is changing, and department and larger stores tend to be more flexible with refunds.

UK SHOPPING IN AUSTRALIA

The internet has made the world a much smaller place, and much of the shopping you may miss from home is available to ship to Australia, albeit you need to shop online.

Next, Amazon, John Lewis, Marks & Spencer, Debenhams, The Book Depository, and House of Fraser are just some of the shops that ship to Australia. Note that not all of the product range is available to ship – policy here is mostly dictated by customs regulations.

Social life

Meeting new acquaintances and forming friendships is undoubtedly a key part of settling into anywhere new. It is also one of the hardest obstacles to overcome and requires a lot of time and effort and a positive, open frame of mind. When in this stage of your arrival to Australia, it's worth repeating this advice. Ensure you refer to the contacts and people you know who are based in Australia – they may be from a previous stage of your life, or have come from introductions through family and friends. Wherever, however, whomever, make sure that you ask around and get introduced no matter how tenuous the link – even if they are not in the city you're intending to settle in. People know people, and you're off to a good start if you have some names of people to meet or connect with when you arrive. They may turn out to be friends or you may not gel with them at all; whatever happens, you never know who else they may be able to introduce you to. The expression 'six degrees of separation' was never more appropriate. This is especially important if you are looking for employment – many jobs here are not advertised, a testament to the power of word of mouth that exists here. Much of the business here relies on strong connections and 'who you know', so it's a case of ensuring your eyes and ears are open at all times.

Being on your best behaviour when meeting new people and trying to make a good impression can be exhausting, but it is so rewarding when you find a bond or commonality that brings you together with a new friend. Meeting new people is hard and requires many of us to step firmly out of our comfort zone. You have nothing to lose in this situation if you don't know anyone – so my advice, no matter how difficult you find it, is to open up, ask for tips, and begin a conversation. Some of your efforts may fall on deaf ears, but, more often than not, you will be greeted with a friendly response and possibly a chat that you can follow up on. Which leads me to my next crucial tip – always follow up, grab a phone number, Facebook friend request, and stay in touch somehow – you never know what after-work drinks or BBQ invite it may lead to.

Many friendships will be forged through work, school, or your interests that involve joining a club or team of some kind. In my experience, having children and/or a pet is extremely helpful when it comes to meeting new people! These may not be desired or indeed possible for many, but they certainly help open up a new world of people with shared interests and priorities. It is crucial to accept every invitation you receive, no matter how little you feel like it or sense that it may not be 'up your alley'. Again, it's a case of 'you never know', so it's always better to put something down to experience than to wonder what may have been or what you are missing.

Inevitably, work and your career will lead you to new connections. You will meet people in your new role, and it is key to make the effort with networking events and communities within your field. Not only is this useful to keep up with new trends and happenings, it is a great way to meet like-minded professionals. If there are clubs or social committees, try volunteering your time, offering to help in some way. This will help to raise your profile, keep you busy, and expose you to new people and experiences.

Hobbies and interests such as sport are a great way to meet new people. Running groups, team sports, joining a band or choir, knitting club, cooking classes, wine appreciation – whatever it may be, with a bit of effort, this is a sure-fire way to meet new people. Perhaps you don't have any hobbies to speak of and you simply enjoy exploring new things – there is a plethora of activities that you would be unlikely to consider back in the UK. Think surfing, paddle boarding, sailing, scuba diving, swimming – all of these are common weekend activities here and you won't be alone when you partake in them.

Last, but certainly not least – the internet has opened up your opportunities to meet new people, including like-minded expats. Many have created blogs to share their experiences, and there are forums where discussions are had about how to overcome certain challenges or deal with situations. The 'Internations' (www.internations.org) community is a thriving global community with a healthy presence in Australia, bringing expats together online, along with regular drinks and parties being held. Meetup (australia.meetup.com) is another way to connect with like-minded people – there are many online groups set up by interest or commonality. It's worth checking out these vibrant and active communities to meet new people and enjoy the best that this country has to offer.

Sports, leisure, and nature

Whether you are an active sports participant or prefer to spectate, you will be well catered for anywhere in Australia.

To join in a sports team or club, a good place to start is with the Australian Sports Commission website. You can search by state and by sport:

www.ausport.gov.au/participating

You won't have to look hard to find a gym, fitness centre, yoga studio, or community centre/pool anywhere in Australia. There are many international gym brands that you will recognise, such as Fitness First and Virgin Active, but also a great range of local and independent gyms available. Some of the following websites can help you:

Gyms: www.localfitness.com.au
Yoga: www.findyoga.com.au
Swimming pools: www.swimming.org/poolfinder

With such beautiful treks and national parks in Australia, bushwalking, swimming, camping, fishing, and sampling local wildlife are all popular pastimes. Parks are managed by state authorities, and can be found at:

ACT: www.tams.act.gov.au/parks-recreation
NSW: www.nationalparks.nsw.gov.au
NT: www.parksandwildlife.nt.gov.au
QLD: www.nprsr.qld.gov.au
SA: www.environment.sa.gov.au/parks/home
TAS: www.parks.tas.gov.au
VIC: parkweb.vic.gov.au
WA: www.dpaw.wa.gov.au

Camping is a popular family choice to get a real flavour of the outdoors. In addition to national parks, head to one of these sites to find sites for your trip:

www.turu.com.au
www.exploreaustralia.net.au/Stay/Campsites#
www.gocampingaustralia.com

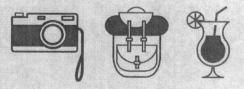

Chapter re-cap – **fun in the sun...**

+ You know more of the lingo and how things work. Now it's time to get out and about, understand the culture, and discover your new home and country.

+ Options are endless for how to spend your leisure time here. There's something for everyone, with an emphasis on being outdoors and socialising.

+ Basics like shopping, knowing where to go for what, and the resources available can help hugely in the settling in period.

+ Socialising, networking, and building a circle of friends is an arduous task. It is essential to make a big effort once you feel more settled.

ADOPTED HOME

Consider this as a state of being or comfort level. The feeling that you are at home and settled as an expat is the pinnacle that we all hope to achieve. Whilst you are not at 'home', you will begin to experience an affinity and bond with Australia that you would miss if you were not here. The feeling of 'being at home' and settled may not be a distinct sense that you will be aware of or recognise. You may have lived in the same place all of your life, so you may not know any different. There are some signs and indications that you are on the way to acclimatising to life here.

Clues that you feel at home:

- ▶ Life feels more natural – generally, things are less of an effort.

- ▶ Nesting is a giveaway – you start to make permanent choices with furniture, you might have bought property, and you may have had children or a pet here.

- ▶ You stop making comparisons between the prices of everything and no longer convert between dollars and £ Sterling.

- ▶ You whinge when the weather isn't perfect.

- ▶ Your Aussie ecosystem matures – you refer to UK news less and less, calls to the UK are less frequent, and you start to develop a social network and have a few people you can count on in Australia.

- ▶ Cultural differences become normal to you; nothing shocks or surprises you anymore.

- ▶ You don't feel like you stand out – you know the ropes, feel comfortable that you know how most things work.

- ▶ Lifelong memories and milestones are created here.

- ▶ You feel distant when you visit the UK, and you look forward to returning home.

- ▶ You know your way around and find yourself knowing where to go for what, rather than having to research each detail.

- ▶ Seeing snow and Christmas trees in shop windows when it's 35°C outside will seem normal.

- ▶ You can't imagine not living here.

- ▶ You can't imagine living back in the UK.

- ▶ The list of requested items you miss from the UK when friends and family come to visit shrinks.

- ▶ Australian citizenship becomes a strong consideration. This is actually straightforward as a UK citizen. Once you have met the time and other requirements, it becomes a case of seeing yourself here for the long haul. The larger conundrum is deciding which nation you'll be supporting at the rugby and cricket!

The list above is not definitive, and you can certainly feel at home by experiencing one or just a few of these. Conversely, you may feel all of the above and still feel like you're not quite as settled as you'd like. Remember that everyone is different, and circumstances and your own subjectivity will determine your comfort levels here. There is no fixed tipping point or one single thing that will happen for this sentiment to materialise.

It's also important to know that there's no fixed timeline associated with this process. Some people, sadly, never feel settled here and will not be happy until they are back on 'home turf' in the UK. The process of adjustment happens over time, and you will likely cross the line into feeling at home without even noticing it.

Depending on your circumstances, and where you are in your Australian, or, indeed, life, journey, you may go through a phase of feeling in limbo. This can be an upsetting process and realisation for some. You will not feel entirely at home or like you belong in Australia, and at the same time will feel an emotional distance from the UK. Basically, neither feels like home and you have a sense that a rug has been pulled from under you. Maybe you've been less communicative with friends from the UK, have started meaningful friendships here, and are still working on the intimacy and bonds to develop closer friendships. This is a good time to re-connect with your UK friendships – these have formed your past and will need effort and work to evolve now that you are on the other side of the world. The truth is that life will go on without you. At the same time, you are creating memories and experiences here that you will be sharing with people here, not the friends you have left behind. Reflect on your time in Australia – perhaps it's time to review and evaluate your life goals. Reaffirm the plans you've made for your future, or realign and rework accordingly.

One thing to consider is your first trip back to the UK. This may be for a specific occasion or a visit once you feel more settled in Australia. It will be exciting to return; you will undoubtedly want to share your experiences, catch up on all of the news that won't have made it onto the Skype or phone calls, and experience a few of the things that you have been missing. It is very likely that your friends and family will marvel at the novelty of your life Down Under, and it will be easy to agree! A word of caution – this trip may unsettle you once you return to Australia. The bonds you have re-formed, if only for a short while, may leave you feeling nostalgic and encourage the sense of limbo. This is normal and will hopefully subside once you return to the routine of your daily life here. This is not to say that you miss your loved ones any less; it's more that you begin to accept the distance as a fact of your new life. The same feelings can be triggered should your friends or family come to visit, and you may experience an empty nest syndrome once they leave. Again, your routine or ticking an item from your wish list can really help.

I experienced the shocking realisation only recently that I have in fact spent most of my life feeling displaced and in a state of limbo. For me, this has meant that nowhere I have ever lived has truly felt like home, but, disturbingly, this was my 'normal'. Before Australia, the longest period spent at the same address was when I was in senior school – a grand total of four years. This possibly contributed to my difficult beginnings here. Naturally, I got itchy feet after our first few years in Australia – with my usual pattern, it was time for a change, and yet I found myself going through this in reverse. Australia was, and is, my home. After all, we had migrated here, became citizens, bought property, and had emotional investment in our friendships here. But I found myself questioning whether my medium-term future was still here. I dabbled with relocating to Asia, got distracted with the feeling that the world was my oyster, and questioned why was I committing so deeply to life here? But, at the end of this, nothing felt more right than staying in Australia. It was extremely peculiar, but I suppose this was further proof that wherever you are in your expat experience in Australia, you may still be wonder what life would be like elsewhere.

Tackling the feeling of displacement is not easy – it can truly be a fork in the road for many. Experiencing life and personal milestones away from the UK and not sharing them with those dearest to you can be difficult, and it's tough not to get sentimental. Especially when you are with friends here that you haven't built a history or trust with yet. There is no right or wrong to what you should be feeling when this happens. It's a case of looking forward and deciding what you want your future to look like. If you decide that you are committed and willing to invest into a life here, simply making this decision will mean that, as time passes, these hurdles will be easier to overcome. This is true if you are here for a fixed length of time or if you are planning to stay here indefinitely. This is a bit of tough love talking, but whichever fork in the road you choose to take is simply a choice. Happiness can be achieved anywhere and with anyone; it's just a matter of what happiness and 'feeling right' looks like to you. This can be life-changing, so be prepared for that, too.

Here are some questions you may wish to ask yourself if you find yourself in limbo. Remember that there are no right or wrong answers, but thinking about them may help in your goal setting:

▶ What is important to me, professionally and personally?

▶ What else do I want to achieve in life?

▶ What can I not live without?

▶ Do I have any regrets in my life so far?

▶ What does happiness look like to me?

Many Brits come to Australia on holiday and never leave – or, like me, take the plunge and never look back. Some cross the line, return to the UK and put the period spent in Australia down to a life-changing experience, settling nicely back into a new life back home. Your time in Australia, whether it is for life, is good, bad, or indifferent, will shape your outlook and mindset for life. No one can take the accomplishment of moving to Australia away from you. Travel has this sneaky habit of changing your perspective, who and how you are as a person, and how the world looks to you. Cherish the experience when and if you leave, and, if you stay, it will be because you have found home. Most importantly, make the most of life here, relish the experience, and you can leave, or continue life here, knowing you have an adopted home.

ACKNOWLEDGEMENTS

...And the Special Thanks go to...

This book would not have been possible without a number of influences and people in my life. Firstly, my husband, Ian, without whom I would not be in Australia, nor as happy as I am with him by my side on the amazing adventures we have taken together. Our application to become Australian residents here was only made possible thanks to two people: Ian, with his great skills and experience in his accomplished IT career, and my Singapore-based Aunt Kuan, who swooped to the rescue when the Australian government inadvertently changed the points requirement and we fell short of the points required to move here. Without her help, our lives would have turned out very differently.

No thanks would be complete without mentioning my parents. My father's determination to provide well for our family took us on a magnificent tour of the world. My mother's unwavering support of my father, brother, and I, along with her guidance, have taught me the value of loyalty and the importance of family, amongst many other values, too many to mention here.

Dillon, our chocolate Lab, must also be mentioned. His antics prove to us daily that laughter really is the best medicine, and his perpetual state of happiness reminds us that life really can be simple.

Last but certainly not least, my nuclear KPI family of Alice, Gareth, Joan, and Sally. You have given me weekly inspiration, motivation, and accountability essential for my sanity, and for that I am so grateful. Not to mention the tremendous laughs along the way. I look forward to your counsel and friendship over the exciting journey ahead. I must also thank the all of the coaches and mentors who have guided my journey – I wouldn't have written this book without them.

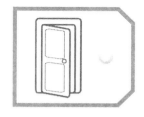

BEFORE YOU GO

Wherever you are on your Australian journey, I hope this book has helped smooth your path. If you have comments or queries, please get in touch at: feedback@soyouremovingto.com.

I have tried to ensure you have the correct web addresses at your fingertips. However, on occasion, these may change. I will keep them up to date on the book's website at www.soyouremovingto.com/booklinks.

If you feel *So, you're moving to Australia?* has been of help to you, please consider leaving a review on Amazon or simply by sending us an email to the address above.

To find out more about the help I provide expat professionals and their families in the crucial planning period and first months of their move to Australia, you can look up The Expat Concierge at: www.theexpatconcierge.com.

Last but certainly not least, be sure to enjoy your travels and adventures!

INDEX

ABOUT THE AUTHOR

Born in Singapore to a British father and Singaporean mother, Sharon has lived anything but a conventional life. Since birth, Sharon has been on the move across five continents, experiencing life and culture in 14 countries over her lifetime so far. Sharon spent her 14 year corporate career working for multinationals including Siemens USA, Abbott Laboratories Germany, Nielsen UK, and WPP's Kantar Australia.

Sharon permanently migrated to Sydney in 2005 with her husband; they are both now Australian citizens. The move was her eighteenth international relocation, and many are amazed to learn that the decision to move Down Under was made without ever visiting Australia.

Unsurprisingly, Sharon's move to Sydney has been the most rewarding and fulfilling one. Sharon has fallen in love with Australia and considers the meticulously planned relocation to Australia her greatest achievement. It did, however, involve more than five years of struggle with the culture change before Australia truly felt like home.

Highly organised and an expert on the Australian lifestyle, Sharon's mission is to ensure expats are fully prepared for the move from the UK and help them settle quickly, feel at home and enjoy their life in Australia. Through her business, The Expat Concierge, Sharon provides hands-on help and guidance to individuals, couples and families who are relocating to Australia.

Sharon lives in Sydney's Inner West with her husband, Ian, and chocolate Labrador, Dillon.

CPSIA information can be obtained at www.ICGtesting.com
Printed in the USA
LVOW11s1610190715

446759LV00023B/339/P